HORÆ ÆGYPTIACÆ:

OR,

THE CHRONOLOGY OF ANCIENT EGYPT

DISCOVERED

FROM ASTRONOMICAL AND HIEROGLYPHIC RECORDS
UPON ITS MONUMENTS;

INCLUDING

MANY DATES FOUND IN COEVAL INSCRIPTIONS FROM THE PERIOD OF THE
BUILDING OF THE GREAT PYRAMID TO THE TIMES OF THE PERSIANS:

AND ILLUSTRATIONS OF

THE HISTORY OF THE FIRST NINETEEN DYNASTIES,
SHEWING THE ORDER OF THEIR SUCCESSION,
FROM THE MONUMENTS.

BY REGINALD STUART POOLE.

ISBN: 978-1-63923-970-2

All Rights reserved. No part of this book maybe reproduced without written permission from the publishers, except by a reviewer who may quote brief passages in a review to be printed in a newspaper or magazine.

Printed: March 2023

Published and Distributed By:
Lushena Books
607 Country Club Drive, Unit E
Bensenville, IL 60106
www.lushenabks.com

ISBN: 978-1-63923-970-2

TO HIS GRACE

ALGERNON DUKE OF NORTHUMBERLAND,

ETC. ETC. ETC.

THIS WORK,

PUBLISHED UNDER HIS GRACE'S AUSPICES,

IS MOST RESPECTFULLY

DEDICATED.

PREFACE.

DURING the last two years of a protracted residence in Egypt, I wrote a series of papers on the Ancient Chronology and History of that country, which have been published in the Literary Gazette. Having returned to England, I began to prepare a new and enlarged edition of those papers; and while I was thus occupied, his Grace the Duke of Northumberland, whose large acquaintance with the monuments of Egypt, and with the science of Egyptian archæology shewed him that much was wanting in my first essay, honoured me by expressing his desire that it should be improved in every way to the utmost of my ability, that the calculations which it contained should be subjected to the most rigid scrutiny, and that illustrations should be unsparingly added. Hence the present volume.

To that distinguished nobleman I owe a large debt of gratitude for the encouragement which he has thus given me; and to several other persons I have to express my acknowledgments for important assistance.

First among these, I must mention my uncle, Mr. Edward William Lane, who has greatly forwarded my undertaking by his most valuable advice and criticism.

I am very deeply indebted to the justly celebrated Sir Gardner Wilkinson, for his having most liberally assisted me, by shewing to me, and allowing me to copy, important inscriptions, &c., in his unpublished papers, and for much valuable information imparted to me in many conversations on most of the subjects treated in this volume. I have also to acknowledge a great favour which he has conferred upon me, in offering to me the use of the wood-blocks from which almost all of the hieroglyphic names of Kings occurring in the present work are printed.

My highly respected and most generous friends, the Rev. Mr. Lieder, of Cairo, and Mrs. Lieder, have forwarded my studies with a zeal that calls for my deepest gratitude. The former has rendered me most important aid in various ways, as will be seen in several of the following pages, in which I have acknowledged my obligations to his extensive learning and his rare liberality. The latter has also afforded me great assistance. I may mention in particular her having lately sent to me a judicious selection of paper-impressions, made with great care, of hieroglyphic inscriptions of much importance, among other acts of kindness too numerous to mention. During the very few occasions of their absence from the scene of their missionary labours, Mr. and Mrs. Lieder have made the necessity for recruiting their health subservient to the cause of researches tending to illustrate and confirm the Bible.

The Astronomer Royal, Mr. Airy, has most obligingly, in compliance with my request, caused calculations which I had previously made to be again made for me at the Royal Observatory, and has revised them himself; a favour for which I cannot be too grateful, as thus I have unquestionable authority for the correctness of data which are among the principal bases of my chronology.

To my kind friend, Mr. A. C. Harris, of Alexandria, a gentleman who deserves the thanks of all students of Egyptian archæology for his contributions to our knowledge of that science, I have to offer my own especial thanks, for his directing my attention to several important hieroglyphic inscriptions, and presenting me with copies of some that I had not seen.

I have also to acknowledge my obligations to Mr. Birch, of the British Museum, for the courtesy and readiness with which he has replied to questions respecting hieroglyphic inscriptions on tablets, &c., under his care; and to Dr. Abbott, of Cairo, for his kindness in permitting me to examine his choice and extensive collection of Egyptian antiquities, and to copy inscriptions contained in it.

REGINALD STUART POOLE.

Hastings, September, 1850.

CONTENTS.

	PAGE
INTRODUCTION	xxi

PART I. CHRONOLOGY.

SECTION I.

THE MONTHS AND YEARS, PROPERLY SO CALLED.

The three Seasons of the Year	3
The Tropical Year	4
The Vague Year	5
Its Antiquity	5
The Names of the Months in Hieroglyphics	6
The earliest known Mention of the Vague Year, in a hieroglyphic Inscription	7
Names of the Months in the Times of the Ptolemies and Cæsars, and in the present Day	7
The Sothic Year	9
The Egyptian Julian Year	9
Symbols of the Year in Hieroglyphics	9

SECTION II.

THE TROPICAL CYCLE.

Description of the Astronomical Ceiling of the Rameseum of El-Kurneh	12
The Symbol of the Autumnal Equinox	14
The Divinities of the Months	14
The Great Ruk-h and the Little Ruk-h	15
The significations of "Ruk-h" in Hieroglyphics, and of the corresponding Words in Coptic	15
The Little Ruk-h shown to be the Vernal Equinox; and the Great Ruk-h, a point of Time a zodiacal Month before that Equinox	16
The Divinities of the Months, continued	18

x   CONTENTS.

                                                                PAGE
Chronological Inscriptions at Benee-Hasan, of the Time of the
    Twelfth Dynasty 18
The Tropical Cycle: its Length and other Characteristics, and
    the Times of its Commencement 20
The Period of the Separate State of the Soul, and its Relation
    to the Tropical Cycle 26

SECTION III.
THE SOTHIC CYCLE.

The Sothic Cycle 28
The Rising of Sothis 29
The Times of the Commencement of the Sothic Cycle . . 32
The Era of Menophrês 33
Osiris, Isis, and Seth 34
The earliest Sothic Cycle 35

SECTION IV.
THE PHŒNIX CYCLE.

The Description of the Astronomical Ceiling of the Rameseum
    of El-Kurneh, resumed 39
Representation of the Phœnix 40
The Period of the Separate State of the Soul, how termed in
    Hieroglyphics 42
The Phœnix Cycle: its Length and other Characteristics, and
    the Times of its Commencement 43
The Sesôstris in whose Time the Phœnix appeared . . 48
The Little Year 50
The Cycle of Twenty-five Years 51
The Fabulous Birds of the Persians and Arabs . . . 51

SECTION V.
THE CALENDAR OF THE DECANS.

Brief explanation of the Calendar of the Decans, and its
    probable Use 53

SECTION VI.
THE CALENDAR OF THE PANEGYRIES.

The " Heb," or " Panegyry ". 55
The Great Panegyrical Month 55

CONTENTS. xi

	PAGE
The Division of the Great Panegyrical Month	56
The Great Panegyrical Year	58
The Date of the Commencement of the Second Great Panegyrical Year in the Time of the two Sûphises	61
The Date of the Commencement of the First Great Panegyrical Year, the Era of Mênês	63
Date in the Time of Skhaï, or Skhee	64
Date in the Time of Queen Amen-numt	65
Another Date in the Time of Queen Amen-numt	66
Date in the Time of Psammetichus II.	67
Date in the Time of Amasis	67
Date in the Tomb of Pet-amen-apt, at Thebes	68

SECTION VII.

THE ROYAL PANEGYRIES.

The Thirty-Year Period of Royal Panegyries	71
The Subdivision of the Thirty-Year Period of Royal Panegyries	73

PART II. HISTORY.

SECTION I.

INTRODUCTORY OBSERVATIONS.

The Order of the First Seventeen Dynasties of Manetho's List	79
Some leading historical Facts relating to those Dynasties	83

SECTION II.

THE LISTS OF MANETHO AND THE MONUMENTS.

A Table of Manetho's List of the First Five Dynasties	86
A Table of Manetho's List of the Sixth and Eleven subsequent Dynasties	88
Remarks on these Tables, and on a Table at the End of the Volume	90
The List of the Chamber of Kings	91
The Tablet of Abydos	91
The Royal Turin Papyrus	92

SECTION III.

HISTORY OF THE PERIOD BEFORE THE SHEPHERD INVASION.

	PAGE
Mênês, the First King of Egypt	93
Notice of the List of Egyptian Kings given by Herodotus (Note)	93
A Remarkable Passage in the Euterpe of Herodotus, respecting the Interval from Mênês to Sethôn	93
The Genesis of the World, marked by the Rising of Sothis, according to Porphyry and Solinus	95
The Era of Mênês ascertained from the Statements of Herodotus, Porphyry, and Solinus, and from the Calendar of the Panegyries	96
The Date of the Dispersion	97
Babylonian and Assyrian Chronology	97
Earliest Median and Persian Kings mentioned in History	98
The Date of the Foundation of Tyre, from Herodotus	98
The Reign of the Gods, Demi-gods, and Manes	99
The History of Mênês	99
Memphis founded by Mênês, according to Herodotus	100
This, and the Thinite Kings	100
A Table shewing the Arrangement of the List called the Tablet of Abydos	101
Explanation of the Tablet of Abydos	102
Athôthis, and the other Kings of the First Dynasty	103
Boêthos, the first King of the Second Dynasty, in whose time an Earthquake happened	104
Animal-worship	105
The second and succeeding Kings of the Second Dynasty	105
The Third Dynasty, the first of Memphite Kings	108
The Fourth Dynasty	109
Erroneous Ideas respecting the Pyramids	109
Contemporaneousness of the Memphites of the Fourth Dynasty with Elephantinites of the Fifth	109
Sôris, Usercherês, and Sephrês; the last of whom founded "the Second Pyramid"	113
Nephercherês	116
The two Sûphises, Shufu, or Sûphis I., and Num-shufu, or Sûphis II.	116
Cheops, or Chembês, the Founder of the Great Pyramid, the Shufu, or Khufu, of the Monuments	118

CONTENTS.

	PAGE
The Chronology of the Period from Mênês to the Sûphises	119
Sisirês	119
Mencherês, the Founder of "the Third Pyramid"	120
The Successors of Mencherês, in the Fourth Dynasty, and of Sisirês, in the Fifth	121
Contemporaneousness of Unas, or Onnos, the last King of the Fifth Dynasty, and Assa, or Assis, the fifth King of the Fifteenth Dynasty	122
Description and Explanation of the List of the Chamber of Kings	124
A Table shewing the Arrangement of the List of the Chamber of Kings	126
A Table comparing the List of the Chamber of Kings with other Lists	128
Explanation of the List of the Chamber of Kings, resumed, shewing the Contemporaneousness of certain Dynasties contained in it	129
The Lists of Chenoboscion	133
The Sixth Dynasty (of Memphites)	133
Tata, or Othoês	134
Papa, or Phiôps: his long Reign	135
Menthesûphis, and Queen Nitôkris	135
Memphis taken by the Shepherds	136
The Ninth Dynasty, the first of Heracleopolite Kings	136
The most probable Chronology of the two Heracleopolite Dynasties, the Ninth and Tenth	138
Achthoês, or Nantef I., the first King of the Ninth Dynasty	138
Nantef II., surnamed "the Great," Nantef III., and Nantef IV.	140
Munt-hotp, the Successor of Nantef IV., shewn to have been contemporary with Amenemha I., the last King of the Eleventh Dynasty	141
A Proof of the partial Contemporaneousness of the Ninth Dynasty with the Eleventh and Twelfth, and with the Fifteenth, deduced from the Names of Persons	142
Similar Proof of the partial Contemporaneousness of the Second, Fourth, Fifth, and other Dynasties, deduced from Kings' Names	143
Account of the Heracleopolite Kingdom, resumed	143
The Eleventh Dynasty, the first of Diospolite Kings	144

xiv CONTENTS.

Amenemha I., or Ammenemês, probably twice deposed, and afterwards restored, contemporary with Munt-hotp, and with a Shepherd-chief 144
The Fourteenth Dynasty, or Xoite Kingdom 147

SECTION IV.

HISTORY OF THE PERIOD OF THE SHEPHERD-DOMINATION.

Chedorlaomer and the Kings confederate with him: their two Invasions of Palestine, the first of which probably caused the Shepherds to invade Egypt 148
Great Famines must have caused many Shepherds to settle in Egypt 150
Probable reasons why the Shepherds so easily subjugated Egypt 150
Manetho's account of the Shepherd-invasion: King Timaios, or Timaos, in whose Reign he says that Event happened . 151
Appellations of the Shepherds: their Race 152
"The Camp of the Tyrians" at Memphis, mentioned by Herodotus 152
Treatment of the conquered Country and People by the Shepherds 153
Great changes in the Egyptian Dynasties, caused by the Shepherd-invasion 154
Chronology of the Twelfth Dynasty (of Diospolites) . . 155
Sesertesen I.: his Power, and the Monuments he has left . 157
Amenemha II. 158
Chronology of the Period from the Súphises to Amenemha II. 159
Differences of Style in Sculptures and Paintings of different Ages 159
Sesertesen II. 161
Sesertesen III., Manetho's Sesôstris 161
Amenemha III., to whom Manetho ascribes the Building of the Labyrinth 161
Contemporaneousness of Amenemha III. with two other Kings, ascertained from an Inscription 162
The Successors of Amenemha III. 163
Chronology of the Shepherd-Dynasties 163
Salatis, the first King of the Fifteenth Dynasty, (of Shepherds,) according to Manetho made Upper and Lower Egypt tributary 166

CONTENTS. XV

PAGE

A proof of the Contemporaneousness of Memphites, Heracleo-
polites, Diospolites, Xoites, and Shepherds, deduced from
the Royal Turin Papyrus, the Lists of Chenoboscion, and
the List of the Chamber of Kings 167
What Eusebius and Africanus say of Salatis, whom they call
Saïtês 169
His Endeavour to preserve his Kingdom from the Assyrians . 169
No authentic Accounts of War between the Assyrians or
Babylonians and the Egyptians in very early Times . . 170
The Foundation of the Frontier-stronghold Avaris by Salatis:
its Position and the Number of its Garrison . . . 170
What is stated in the Lists of Africanus and Eusebius respect-
ing the Shepherd-invasion 171
Abraham's Visit to Egypt 172
Ra-snufre Pi-ankhee, or Bêôn, the second King of the Fif-
teenth Dynasty 172
An Evidence of the Contemporaneousness of the Twelfth and
Fifteenth Dynasties 173
Apachnas 174
Aan, or Iannas 174
Assa, or Assis, ruled not only Memphis, but also Leontopolis,
or the Leontopolite Nome 175
Aphôbis or Apôphis 177
The early Greek Traditions 178
Supposed Time of the Foundation of the Kingdoms of Sicyon
and Argos 178
Connexion between Greece and Egypt 178
The Pelasgi 178
The Thirteenth Dynasty (of Diospolites) 179
The Fourteenth Dynasty (of Xoites) 181
The Seventh and Eighth Dynasties (of Memphites) . . 181
Etymology of the Name "Hyksôs," and origin of the Shepherds 182
Length of the Shepherd-rule, according to Manetho, and Insur-
rection against the Shepherds 183
Migrations from Egypt to Greece 184
" Cecrops the Saïte " and Cadmus 185
Danaus and Ægyptus 186
Curious Traditions relating to the Colonizers of Greece, from
Strabo, Agatharchides, and Diodorus Siculus . . . 186

SECTION V.

HISTORY OF THE PERIOD OF THE EIGHTEENTH AND NINETEENTH DYNASTIES.

	PAGE
Power of the Pharaohs of the Eighteenth and Nineteenth Dynasties	188
Table of Manetho's Lists of the Eighteenth and Nineteenth Dynasties	189
Enumeration of the Kings of the Eighteenth and Nineteenth Dynasties, and notice of certain Corrections and Alterations in Manetho's Lists of those Dynasties	190
Chronology of the Eighteenth and Nineteenth Dynasties	198
The Reign of Queen Amen-numt	198
The Exodus of the Shepherds	199
The King of the Shepherd-Exodus	201
The Sun-worshippers in Egypt	201
The Eastern Ethiopians	202
The Kings of the Sun-worshippers in Egypt	203
Sun-worship	204
Hor-em-heb, doubtless the King who overcame the Sun-worshippers	206
Nature of the Inquiry contained in the Second Part of this Work	207
Concluding Remarks	209

APPENDIX.

Letter from the Astronomer Royal	215
Hieroglyphic Tables of Kings	218
Hieroglyphic Table of the First Seventeen Dynasties	219
Hieroglyphic Table of the Eighteenth and Nineteenth Dynasties	253
Some Names of unplaced Kings, and some Variations of the Names of placed Kings	261

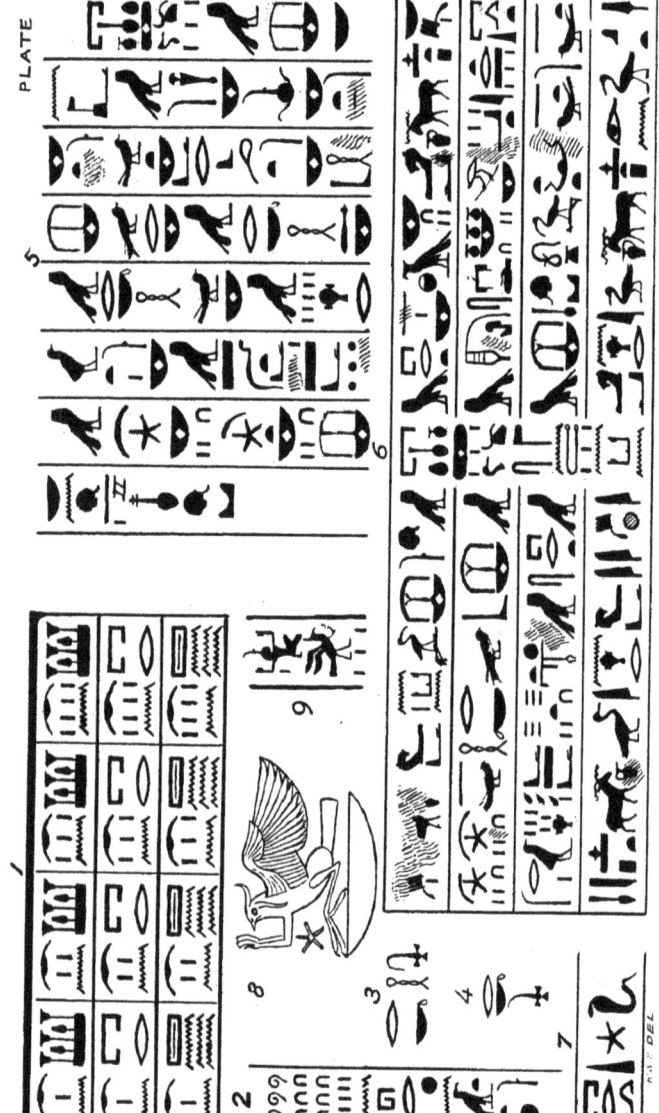

PLATE II

DESCRIPTION OF PLATES.

PLATE I.

1. Hieroglyphic names of the Seasons and Months. See p. 3.
2. Mention of the 365 days of the Vague Year, in an inscription on a box of the time of Amenoph I. (B.C. cir. 1500), in the Turin Museum. From an unpublished copy by Sir Gardner Wilkinson. See p. 7.
3 & 4. Name of Ruk-h. See p. 15.
5. Portion of the long inscription in the tomb of Num-hotp, at Benee-Hasan, containing a record of the commencement of the first Tropical Cycle, B.C. 2005, in the reign of Amenemha II. See pp. 18, 19.
6. Inscription over the door of the same tomb. See p. 19.
7. "Manifestation of Sothis." See p. 31.
8. Fabulous bird, symbolizing a pure soul. See p. 42.
9. Extract from the inscriptions of the sarcophagus of Queen Ankh-nes, in the British Museum, mentioning the cycle of the separate state of the soul. See p. 42.

PLATE II.

The most remarkable portions of the astronomical ceiling of the Rameseum of El-Kurneh; containing representations of the Phœnix (see p. 39), Sothis (see p. 28), the constellation Taurus, &c. (see p. 41), the two Ruk-hs (see p. 15), and the sitting Cynocephalus (see p. 14), in the following order:—

The Phœnix.   Sothis.
              Taurus, &c.
The Great Ruk-h.   The Cynocephalus.   The Little Ruk-h.

PLATE III.

1, 2, 3, & 4. Different modes of writing the "Great Panegyrical Month." See p. 55.
5, 6, 7, 8, & 9. Different modes of writing the "Division of the Great Panegyrical Month." See p. 56.
10. "The Great Panegyrical Month of Smat," from an inscription in a tomb near the Pyramids of El-Geezeh. See pp. 60, 61.

xviii DESCRIPTION OF PLATES.

11. "Smat, the star of the Division of the Great Panegyrical Month," from the astronomical ceiling of the Rameseum of El-Kurneh. See p. 57.

12. Record of the commencement of the second Great Panegyrical Year B.C. 2352, with the name of Num-shufu, of the Fourth Dynasty; from a tomb near the Great Pyramid. See p. 61.

13. Record of a date of the Sixth Great Panegyrical Month, the Fifteenth Division of the Great Panegyrical Month, B.C. 1451 or 1450; from a tomb at Thebes. See p. 65.

14. Part of an inscription at Gebel-es-Silsileh, in Upper Egypt, recording the commencement of periods of Royal Panegyries in the thirtieth, thirty-fourth, thirty-seventh, and fortieth, years of the reign of Rameses II.; from Champollion's "Monumens," Plate 116. See p. 73.

15 & 16. "Heb," the common name of the ancient Egyptian religious festivals, "a Panegyry." See p. 55.

Plate IV.

1. The list of Kings comprised in the Tablet of Abydos. See p. 101.

2. List of three Kings' names, from a tomb near the Pyramids of El-Geezeh. See p. 111.

3. List of four Kings' names (two of which are of the same King), from a tomb near the Pyramids of El-Geezeh. See p. 111.

4. List of five Kings' names, from a tomb near the Pyramids of El-Geezeh. See pp. 106, 112.

Plate V.

Inscription in a tomb near the Great Pyramid, shewing the contemporaneousness of Unas, of the Fifth Dynasty, with Assa, of the Fifteenth; from the Rev. Mr. Lieder and Mrs. Lieder. See p. 122.

Plate VI.

The List of Kings comprised in "the Chamber of Kings." See p. 124.

Plate VII.

1. Fragment of the Royal Turin Papyrus. See p. 167.

2. The same in hieroglyphic characters.

3. One of the Lists of Chenoboscion, from a tomb at that place. See p. 167.

PLATE IV.

PLATE V.

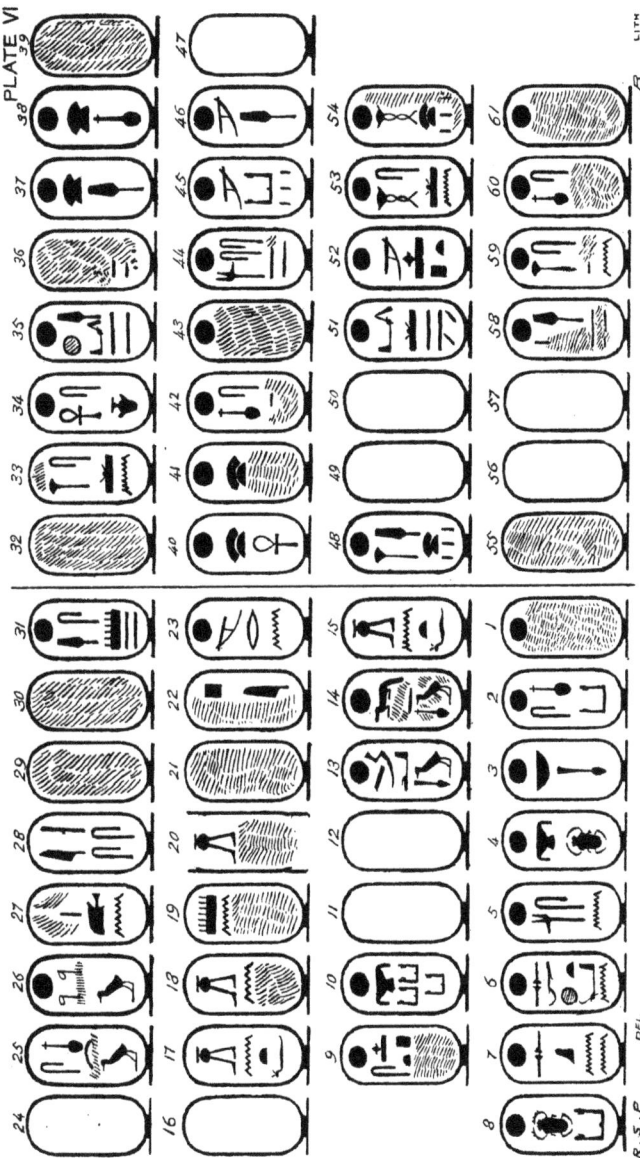

PLATE VI

PLATE VII

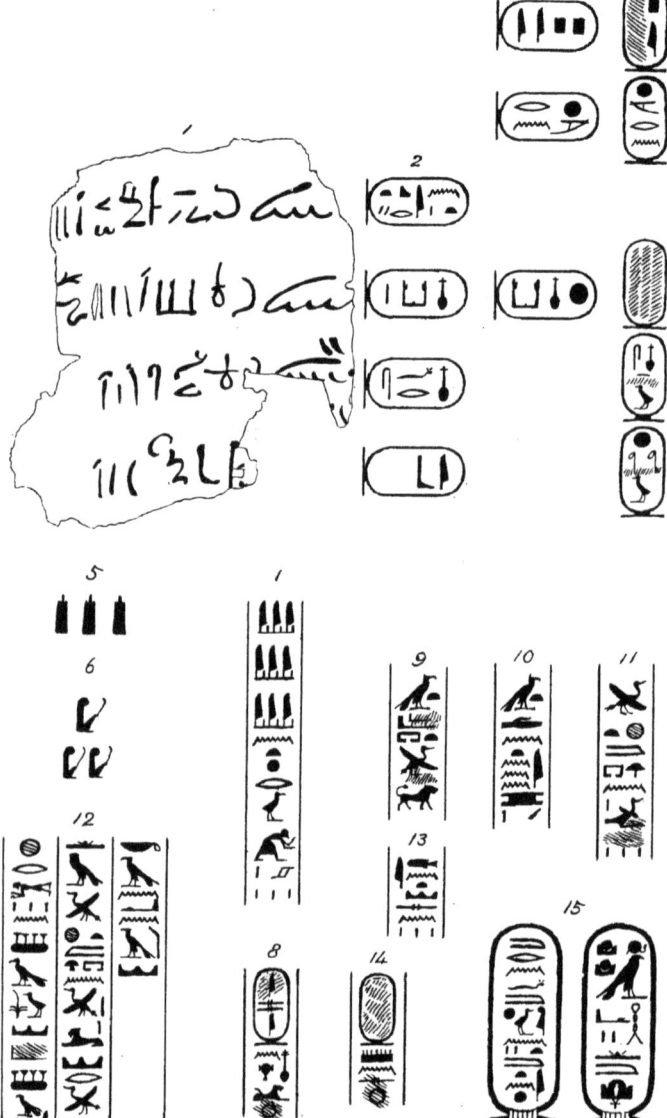

DESCRIPTION OF PLATES. xix

4. Extract from the List of the Chamber of Kings. See p. 167.

5. Name of a foreign race, which probably reads Penu, or Phœnicians. See pp. 146, 153.

6. "Shepherds." See p. 153.

7. Mention of the Shepherds, here called enemies, or foreigners, and of the Fields, probably the Bucolia, from the long inscription in the tomb of Num-hotp, at Benee-Hasan. See pp. 153, 174.

8. Inscription of the time of Assa, of the Fifteenth Dynasty, making mention of the City or Land of the Lion, that is, of Leontopolis or the Leontopolite Nome. See p. 176.

9. "City of the Lion," from one of the sculptures of Sethee I., on the exterior of the north wall of the great temple of El-Karnak, at Thebes. See p. 176.

10. Name of a branch of the Nile, from the same sculpture. See p. 176.

11. Fortress on that branch of the Nile, from the same sculpture. See p. 176.

12. Part of an inscription, accompanying another sculpture of Sethee I., also on the exterior of the north wall of the great temple of El-Karnak, mentioning foreigners, or enemies, expelled from Egypt, by that King. See pp. 153, 176.

13. Mention of the land of A-ant, from the same inscription. See p. 176.

14. Mention of Saïs, from the tomb containing No. 8. See p. 177.

15. Names of Aten-ra, the god of the Sun-worshippers. See p. 204.

ERRATA.

Page 21, *insert* the figures 2 and 4 *over* the second and fourth pairs of names in this page.

„ 33, line 10, *for* "Men-path" *read* "Men-ptah."

„ 82, line 5, *for* "presently" *read* "hereafter."

„ 117, last line, *for* "my friend" *read* "another friend."

„ 121, line 6 from bottom, *for* "doubtless" *read* "apparently."

„ 123, line 11, *for* "sums" *read* "sum."

„ 140, line 8 from bottom, *insert* "certainly" *after* "been."

„ 143, note *, line 2 from bottom, *after* "and" *insert* "that it."

„ 144, line 9 from bottom, *for* "ings" *read* "Kings."

„ 149, line 3, *for* "dwell" *read* "dwelt."

„ 178, line 6 from bottom, *for* "Palestine" *read* "Phœnicia."

„ 231, column 4, *dele* "II." *after* "Munt-hotp."

INTRODUCTION.

THE object of the present work is to explain the Chronology and History of Ancient Egypt from its monuments. It is divided into two parts. The first part is an examination of the ancient Egyptian divisions of time, and the dates recorded on the monuments. The second part is an inquiry into the history of the first nineteen Dynasties, and an application of the chronology obtained in the preceding part to that history.

I may be permitted here to state the circumstances which led me to write this work. At the time when I began to study hieroglyphics in Egypt, from the monuments, and from the works of Champollion and others, I found that the learned world deplored the want of monumental evidence by which to fix the chronology of the ancient Egyptian Dynasties, and to determine whether any of them were contemporary or not. On considering the possibility of finding this much-desired evidence, I saw that I needed not to despair of finding it myself. It is true that others, for whose learning I have the highest respect, had not met with success in similar endeavours; but I was more favourably situated than most of those who had preceded me; having my time unoccupied by any other important scientific or literary pursuit, excepting a course of general study, which assisted me in my progress; and the monuments were near to be consulted. How far I have succeeded in my attempt, the following pages will show. If any one suppose that I have been guided by prejudice, I can only reply to him by asserting that the results of my investigations have been wholly unexpected to me, as I shall have occasion more explicitly to show.

I have avoided, as much as possible, quoting or examining the works of others, excepting Sir Gardner Wilkinson. My object has been to explain what I have learned from the monuments; not to combat the assertions of others. Sir Gardner Wilkinson stands in a position different from that of any others who have written on the subject; he has never written to support a chronological hypothesis, and is entitled to the utmost confidence on account of his well-known accuracy, the many years which he has spent in the study of the Egyptian monuments in Egypt, and the caution which he has shown in refraining from putting forth any complete system of Egyptian chronology*. I am aware how greatly I disagree with all others who have written on this subject; but

* Since my work has been written, I have read, with no little pride, the following words in his latest publication, his very interesting and beautiful work on the Architecture of Ancient Egypt. After some remarks on the subject of chronology, he says, "It is indeed less necessary to enter into a detailed exami-

it is a sufficient consolation to me, since all differ, that it is little more to differ from all others than to differ from all of them but one.

I must beg the reader to bear in mind throughout, that nothing inconsistent with the unquestionable records of the monuments has formed any part of the foundation upon which I have built.

"I speak as to wise men; judge ye what I say."

nation of the chronology, and the succession of the Pharaohs, as Mr. Stuart Poole's work on the subject will soon be published; and I have much pleasure in stating how fully I agree with him in the contemporaneousness of certain kings, and in the order of succession he gives to the early Pharaohs."—p. 132.

HORÆ ÆGYPTIACÆ.

PART I.
CHRONOLOGY.

SECTION I.

THE MONTHS AND YEARS, PROPERLY SO CALLED.

THE Egyptians, from very early times, subdivided the year which they commonly used into three seasons, each containing four months, called the first, second, third, and fourth, months of those seasons. This notation evidently obtained from the very earliest times of Egyptian history. The three seasons were called "the Season of Vegetation," "the Season of Manifestation," and "the Season of the Waters," or the "Inundation." * There are diversities of opinion respecting the interpretation of the names of the first two seasons; and what I have given as the interpretation of the name of the second season is merely the radical signification of the group; but the name of the third season is undoubtedly "the Season of the Waters," and this gives us an accurate means of ascertaining the characteristics of that tropical year to which these names of the seasons must have originally applied. The fitness of this division is shown by our finding it universally used in Egypt in the present day, though vaguely defined; the three seasons being called الشتاء "Winter," الصيف "Summer," and النيل "the Inundation," literally "the Nile," meaning the season

* The hieroglyphic names of the seasons and months are given in Plate I., No. 1.

at which the Nile is spread over the cultivable parts of Egypt.

"The Season of the Waters," in the ancient nomenclature, plainly shows that the Tropical Year to which that nomenclature was originally applied commenced at the winter solstice, and not at, nor near, either of the equinoxes, or the summer solstice. We find in the present day that the four months during which the Nile is higher than at any other period of the year commence (according to the most accurate modern observations) almost exactly a month and a half before the autumnal equinox, and terminate almost exactly two months and a half after the same equinox. But the inundation commences almost exactly a month before the equinox, sometimes a few days earlier, sometimes a few days later; and it continues somewhat longer than it naturally would do, because the waters are retained for some time upon the lands by closing the mouths of the canals. We find, also, by the Egyptian almanacs, that, according to a tradition handed down by the Copts, what is called "the Bridal of Nilus" (from an unfounded legend, that on this occasion a virgin was thrown into the Nile as a sacrifice), which is the ceremony of the cutting of the dam which closes the mouth of the Canal of Cairo, formerly called the Amnis Trajanus, took place, in ancient times, exactly one month before the autumnal equinox. Now, it is by this operation that the inundation is allowed to commence, the water being previously confined between its banks, and no other canals being suffered to be before opened to admit the water upon the lands. The Canal of Cairo is now generally cut about a fortnight too early, on account of an old law, which forbids the levying of the land-tax unless the river rise to the height of sixteen cubits; and, therefore, they assert it to have done so before such is really the case. Thus we find that the true period of the commencement of "the Season of the Inundation" was one month before the autumnal equinox; and the end, at the winter solstice; and, consequently, that the Tropical Year anciently in use among the Egyptians commenced at the winter solstice, when all things in Egypt begin anew.

The Egyptians had also, in very early times, a year consisting of 365 days, apparently more ancient than the Tropical Year, and consecrated by its antiquity. This year is commonly called "the Vague Year," and was subdivided into twelve months of thirty days each, with an addition of five Epagomenæ, or intercalary days, after the twelfth month. The great simplicity of this year shows its antiquity. It appears to me most probable that it was instituted shortly after the time of the Deluge (following Hales's Chronology); for I find strong reasons for supposing that, at the time of its institution, it commenced with the autumnal equinox, which would have been the case at that time. In the astronomical sculptures of the Rameseum of El-Kurneh, we find a symbol of the autumnal equinox represented as one of the divinities of the first month; and, in like manner, a symbol of the vernal equinox as the god of the seventh month. If the Vague Year were instituted at the remote period which I have mentioned, we may reasonably suppose that they who instituted it imagined that the division of that year into two periods, one of six months, and the other of six months and five days, corresponded to the natural division of a tropical year, commencing with the autumnal equinox. Probably the first colonizers of Egypt brought the Vague Year from the land of Shinar, and instituted the Tropical Year on their settlement in a country of such marked physical phenomena. We find the Vague Year to have been in common use, judging from the inscriptions, at least as early as the time of the Eighteenth Dynasty, in the fourteenth and fifteenth centuries B.C.; and we find its months constantly receiving the same hieroglyphic appellations as the months of the Tropical Year. Thus, the first month of the Vague Year is called "the first month of the Season of Vegetation," and so on. This suggests an interesting inquiry as to when these names were first applied in this manner; but such an inquiry can lead to no satisfactory result. If any suppose that this happened when the Vague and Tropical Years coincided, which was the case in the year B.C. 2005—a year signalized by the commencement of a great period—let him consider that the Egyptians had, by a sufficiently long experience, ascertained that the coincidence could not continue. If he imagine that there was a preceding coincidence, and that at that coincidence the double application of the names was made by the Egyptians (supposing the Egyptian nation then to have existed), he must not only run counter to all genuine history and tradition, but must attribute to the ancient Egyptians an inconceivable ignorance of astronomy; since, in doing thus, they would have shown themselves ignorant of the relative lengths of the Vague and Tropical Years, and the only persons who could advocate such an idea as that the Egyptians instituted their Vague Year about 3500 B.C. are the very persons who attribute to them, at that ideal period of their existence, a profound knowledge of astronomy.

Sir Gardner Wilkinson has pointed out to me the earliest decided instance hitherto found of the mention of the Vague Year, in an inscription of the time of Amenoph I., the second King of the Eighteenth

Dynasty, in the Turin Museum, of which he kindly permitted me to make a copy, from his own. The mention of the 365 days of the year I insert in one of the plates accompanying this volume. (Plate I., No. 2.) Some have supposed that the Egyptian year was originally lunar. Of this I have found no evidence upon the monuments.

The names by which the Egyptian months were called (excepting in hieroglyphic inscriptions) in the times of the Ptolemies and Cæsars—Thôth, or Thôÿth, Paôphi, &c.—are never found (as such) in hieroglyphics of any time. We shall presently see that they were chiefly, or wholly, derived from the names of the divinities to which the months were considered sacred.

The following are the names of the Egyptian months in the Memphitic dialect, in the first column; according to the modern Egyptian pronunciation, in the second column; and in Greek, in the third column: in each case I have given what appears to me to be the most common mode of writing:—

EGYPTIAN MONTHS. [Part I.

1. ⲐⲰⲞⲨⲦ	توت	Θώθ.	
Thôüt.	Toot.	Thôth.	
2. ⲠⲀⲰⲠⲒ	بابه	Παωφὶ.	
Paôpi.	Bábeh.	Paôphi.	
3. ⲀⲐⲰⲢ	هاتور	Ἀθὺρ.	
Athôr.	Hátoor.	Athyr.	
4. ⲬⲞⲒⲀⲔ	كيهك	Χοιάκ.	
Choiak.	Kiyahk.	Choiak.	
5. ⲦⲰⲂⲒ	طوبه	Τυβὶ.	
Tôbi.	Toobeh.	Tybi.	
6. ⲘⲈⲬⲒⲢ	امشير	Μεχὶρ.	
Mechir.	Amsheer.	Mechir.	
7. ⲪⲀⲘⲈⲚⲰⲐ	برمهات	Φαμενὼθ.	
Phamenôth.	Barmahát.	Phamenôth.	
8. ⲪⲀⲢⲘⲞⲨⲐⲒ	برموده	Φαρμουθὶ.	
Pharmuthi.	Barmoodeh.	Pharmuthi.	
9. ⲠⲀⲬⲰⲚ	بشنس	Παχὼν.	
Pachôn.	Beshens.	Pachôn.	
10. ⲠⲀⲰⲚⲒ	بوونه	Παϋνὶ	
Paôni.	Ba-ooneh.	Paÿni.	
11. ⲈⲠⲎⲠⲒ	ابيب	Ἐπιφὶ.	
Epêpi.	Ebeeb.	Epiphi.	
12. ⲘⲈⲤⲰⲢⲎ	مسري	Μεσορὶ.	
Mesôrê.	Misra.	Mesori.	

The names in the second column are almost exactly the same in sound as those which we find in books in the Sahidic dialect. The ninth month is called, in the Sahidic dialect, ⲡⲁϣⲟⲛⲥ (Pashons) and ⲡⲁϣⲱⲛⲥ (Pashôns); and this, combined with the hieroglyphics, shows that the proper mode of writing it in the Memphitic dialect is ⲡⲁⲭⲱⲛⲥ (Pachôns), and, in Greek, Παχὼνς.

When the Sothic Year, or year which commenced at the rising of Sothis, was first instituted, I think extremely doubtful; and hitherto I have found it of no use in the application of Egyptian chronology to history. It was probably a year of the priests, used only in times long subsequent to the foundation of the Egyptian kingdom, at least not long before the first Sothic Cycle, which commenced B.C. 1322. It seems to me not improbable that it was then instituted. Its length was the same as that of the Julian.

When Egypt had become a province of the Roman empire, Augustus commanded the Egyptians to make use of a Julian year in their public records. But instead of making its commencement the same as that of the common Julian Year, the Egyptians made the Vague Year Julian by intercalation; consequently, the Egyptian Julian Year always commenced on the 29th, or, in the year next after their leap-year, the 30th, of August, O.S., which was the day on which the Vague Year commenced, B.C. 24, when the new reckoning began. The Copts and the Egyptian peasants still make use of this year.

In hieroglyphics, the symbol of the year was a palm-branch, stripped of its leaves, and with one notch.

The most common group, signifying "year," is composed of this symbolic sign, followed by the sign of the feminine gender, and the restrictive adjunct of solar divisions of time*. It is worthy of remark, that the Arabs make use of a palm-branch stripped of its leaves as a tally by which to keep accounts; and they use the term جَرِيدَة, *jereedeh*, the name of such a palm-branch, to signify a register; and the Persians and Turks make use of that word in a similar manner. This, combined with the fact that we find the gods often represented marking the number of the festivals of the King on a palm-branch with many notches, is sufficient to explain the reason why a palm-branch was chosen for the symbol of the year. Horapollo Nilous says, with reference to this symbol of the year, after having noticed another symbol, "Representing the year otherwise, they delineate a palm-tree, because this tree only, unlike all other trees, at the rising of the moon, [that is, at each new moon,] produces one branch, so that in twelve branches the year is completed." (Καὶ ἑτέρως δὲ ἐνιαυτὸν γράφοντες, φοίνικα ζωγραφοῦσι, διὰ τὸ δένδρον τοῦτο μόνον τῶν ἄλλων κατὰ τὴν ἀνατολὴν τῆς σελήνης, μίαν βάϊν γεννᾶν, ὡς ἐν ταῖς δώδεκα βάϊσιν ἐνιαυτὸν ἀπαρτίζεσθαι†.) And again, in the next chapter, he says, Μῆνα δὲ γράφοντες, βάϊν ζωγραφοῦσιν, κ. τ. λ.‡ I have not, however, found a palm-tree represented as the symbol of a year, nor a palm-branch as the symbol of a month; but I have found the many-notched palm-branch used to signify "year" in an inscription of the

---

* See Plate I., No. 2, last three characters.
† Hieroglyphics of Horapollo Nilous, Ed. Cory., pp. 9, 10.
‡ Id. p. 10.

time of Sesertesen I.*, the first King of the Twelfth Dynasty.

It is remarkable that the Egyptians called a cycle "a year," or "a great year," and symbolized it by a palm-branch; and that the Greeks called the Phœnix and the palm-tree by the same name, $\Phi o\hat{\iota}\nu\iota\xi$.

* The name of this king will be found a few pages later. The value of the first character in it is doubtful; and hence it has been also read Osirtesen, and Osortasen, and Usrtesen; but I have lately found a strong reason for believing the value of the character in question to be "S."

SECTION II.

THE TROPICAL CYCLE.

ONE of the most interesting of the monuments of ancient Egypt is the great temple erected by Rameses II., the second King of the Nineteenth Dynasty,

according to Manetho's division, on the western side of the Nile, at Thebes. It is commonly called "the Memnonium;" but this is an inappropriate appellation, and I prefer calling it "the Rameseum of El-Kurneh." "Rameseum" is the proper name of every building erected by a Rameses; and "El-Kurneh" is the modern name of the district in which the temple stands. Among the sculptures of this edifice is one which has deservedly been regarded by the learned as of very great importance. I allude to the famous astronomical ceiling of one of its apartments*. This has been shown to be a record of great value, as affording us means of judging of the astronomical knowledge of the ancient Egyptians at the early period at which it was sculptured, and as indicating, approximatively, the time

---

* See Plate II.

of the reign of Rameses II.; but beyond this, I know not of its having hitherto conveyed any useful information to the chronologer or historian. A careful examination, however, has shown me that it affords data for fixing other points of the ancient Egyptian chronology, especially that of the earlier dynasties, respecting which the most approved writers have so greatly differed, that some have placed particular dynasties about a thousand years higher than others.

The ceiling above mentioned is of an oblong form, and contains three principal longitudinal divisions, surrounded by a narrow border of hieroglyphics. Certain portions of its first division exhibit the coincidence of points of a Vague Year with certain astronomical phenomena, and part of the second division relates to the same subject. The upper part of the first division is occupied by a narrow subdivision, running through its entire length, and divided into thirteen spaces, twelve of which have the names of the Egyptian months inscribed in them, the thirteenth being left vacant for the Epagomenæ, or five intercalary days. This vacant space occupies the central position; the spaces from it to the left extremity of the ceiling containing the names of the first six months, from Thoth to Mechir inclusive; and those from the right extremity to it, the names of the other six months, from Phamenoth to Mesori. The third division contains representations of the divinities to which the months were consecrated, and of the King performing acts of worship to those divinities. This division I propose first to examine. Before commencing this examination, I must, however, remark, that the sculptures of the first division, compared with other monumental data, show us that the ceiling was sculptured in some one of the first 120 years of the first Sothic Cycle, B.C. 1322 to 1202; and it is most probable (as will be shown in the course of this work) that the former of those dates fell in the reign of the immediate predecessor of Rameses II. The third division, like the two others, contains several subdivisions. Commencing our examination from that part which is beneath the space of the Epagomenæ, we find a subdivision which corresponds to that space, and contains a figure of a cynocephalus, the emblem of the god Thoth, seated on what some have supposed to be a Nilometer. Horapollo says, that a sitting cynocephalus denoted the two equinoxes. (Ἰσημερίας δύο πάλιν σημαίνοντες, κυνοκέφαλον καθήμενον ζωγραφοῦσι ζῷον.)* It is evident, however, that although a sitting cynocephalus denoted the two equinoxes in the time of Horapollo, according to that author's statement, yet it denoted but one in the time of Rameses II., from its occurring but once in this representation of the year. After an interval of six months, we find a figure which undoubtedly represents the vernal equinox; and, consequently, the cynocephalus represents the autumnal equinox†.

After the figure of the sitting cynocephalus, we find ten figures of different divinities, and two emblems of physical phenomena, here regarded as divinities, corresponding in number to the twelve months, and being the divinities to which the months were consecrated, and from which they chiefly took their names. We must, however, reckon the divinities of the months as thirteen, allotting two to the first month; for the em-

* Hieroglyphics of Horapollo Nilous, Ed. Cory., p. 36.

† It is well known that, during the interval from the Nineteenth Dynasty to the time at which Horapollo wrote, hieroglyphics had been much corrupted.

blem of the autumnal equinox should be included in their number, like that of the vernal equinox, especially as it is also the emblem of Thoth, the god of letters, from whom the first month evidently took its name. The next subdivision to that in which is the cynocephalus, contains two figures of the King, standing in an attitude of worship before two divinities. The first of these is goddess of the month of Thoth, which is thus shown to have been consecrated to two divinities. The god of the second month is Ptah, or Phthah, whence probably its name, Paophi, or Pa-ptah, that is, "the month of Ptah." The next subdivision contains figures of the King and of At-hor and Pasht, or Pakht, the goddesses of Athyr and Choiak. Then we find a representation of Khem, the god of Tybi. Beneath the sixth and seventh months, Mechir and Phamenoth, we find two figures of jackals, called, respectively, Ruk-h Ur, and Ruk-h Se, or "the Great Ruk-h," and "the Little Ruk-h."* The latter name might be supposed to read "the Son of the Ruk-h," if we did not find it written in other cases "the Little Ruk-h," in a manner that cannot admit of a different interpretation. The hieroglyphic names may be seen in the sketch of the ceiling of the Rameseum of El-Kurneh, and some variations will be found in the copies of inscriptions in other plates in this work. The significations of Ruk-h, according to Champollion, are "heat," "to burn," and "a live coal." The restrictive adjunct is a small pot, or other vessel, from which a flame issues †. In Coptic we find that several words with the radicals ⲣ, ⲕ, ⳉ, have the same significations. ⲣⲟⲕⳉ signifies "burn-

* See Plate II.
† See two forms of writing "Ruk-h" with this restrictive adjunct, in Plate I., Nos. 3 and 4.

ing, consumption, fuel; to burn, to be burnt," &c. ⲣⲱⲕϩ in like manner signifies "a fire, heat, firewood; to burn, to inflame," &c. ⲡⲉⲕϩ signifies "to burn." ⲡⲁⲕϩⲉ signifies "a live coal," &c.; and ⲡⲁⲕϩⲓ, "firewood," and, in the plural, "live coals." On comparing these significations with those of the hieroglyphic word Ruk-h, we see that its proper meaning was "a live coal," and its tropical meaning, "burning," or "to burn," and thence "heat." I have been thus particular in explaining the various significations of Ruk-h in hieroglyphics, on account of the great importance of a fact which I shall have soon to state as one of the proofs of the identity of the second Ruk-h with the vernal equinox.

I have now to observe, first, that the places of the two Ruk-hs in relation to the place of the cynocephalus, which I have shown to represent one of the two equinoxes, suggest that the Second (or Little) Ruk-h also represents an equinox. Secondly, the modern Egyptians call the vernal equinox "esh-Shems el-Kebeereh" الشمس الكبيرة or "the Great Sun," and a point of time exactly a zodiacal month before that equinox, "esh-Shems es-Sagheereh" الشمس الصغيرة or "the Little Sun." These two names are vulgarly pronounced "esh-Shems el-Kebeer," and "esh-Shems es-Sugheiyir." This I consider sufficient to show what are the two Ruk-hs, notwithstanding that the Great Ruk-h precedes the Little, and the Little Sun precedes the Great; for the ancient Egyptians may have had as good a reason for calling the First Ruk-h "great" as the modern Egyptians have for applying that epithet to the Second Sun. But to prove that the Great Ruk-h is identical with the Little Sun, I proceed to observe, thirdly, that the point of time called the Little Sun is

THE VERNAL EQUINOX.

also called, in the modern Egyptian almanacs, *by a name exactly agreeing with the appellation of* "*First Ruk-h*," namely, "el-Jemreh el-Oolà," الجمرة الأولي that is, "the First Live Coal." This must satisfy every one as to the identity of the First Ruk-h with the Little Sun; and the Second Ruk-h is doubtless the Great Sun, although the point of time called the Great Sun is not called, by the modern Egyptians, "the Second Live Coal;" for they have three "live coals;" the second of which is seven days after the first; and the third, seven days after the second. The three "live coals" are described as being three degrees of warmth or heat; so that Ruk-h and Jemreh signify both a live coal, and a particular degree of heat at a particular season of the year. But even this is not all the evidence we have of the identity of the First (or Great) Ruk-h with the period called by the modern Egyptians the Little Sun, and of the Second (or Little) Ruk-h with the Great Sun, or vernal equinox. In the list of the gods of the months in the great temple of Adfoo, or Apollinopolis Magna, we find, in three cases, the names of divinities followed by the word "Panegyry" (or festival), showing that the Panegyries of these divinities were celebrated during the months sacred to them. This is the case with the Great Ruk-h; for, instead of "the Great Ruk-h," as in the Rameseum of El-Kurneh, we find written "Ruk-h Ur Heb," that is, "the Panegyry of the Great Ruk-h;" and thus we find that the Panegyry of the Great Ruk-h was celebrated in Mechir at the time when this record was made. Now it was made in the reign of Ptolemy Euergetes II., in whose reign, after an interval of about 1500 years from a preceding coincidence of the same kind, the Great Ruk-h began again to fall in Mechir, and the Little Ruk-h in Phamenoth. Such a coincidence, as I have before shown, most probably marked the institution of the Vague Year; and probably the record of Ptolemy was sculptured as a commemoration of a recurrence of this coincidence. Thus I have adduced evidence more than sufficient to establish the point in question.

To return to the subject of the divinities of the months. Under the month of Pharmuthi, the King is represented offering incense to the goddess Ren-nu. We next see him standing in an attitude of worship before Khuns, the god of Pachon, as the Greeks wrote the name of the ninth month, which should be written Pachons, that is, Pa-Khuns, "belonging to Khuns." The King is next represented standing before Fen-tee, the god of Payni; and then, making an offering to the goddess of Epiphi, who has a name that I cannot read with certainty; and, lastly, to Ra, the god of Mesori. The name of the last month is probably derived from Mes-ra, the hieroglyphic name of the constellation Taurus.

The identification of the two Ruk-hs has led me to the discovery of a most important cycle, which fixes with exactitude certain points in the ancient Egyptian chronology.

In the celebrated sepulchral grottoes of Benee-Hasan, in Middle Egypt, are two hieroglyphic inscriptions of the time of the Twelfth Dynasty, which partly relate to a commencement of the great period just mentioned. I give, in Plate I., Nos. 5 and 6, correct copies, made by me on the spot, of so much of these inscriptions as relates to the subject of which I am now treating. The first extract reads thus:—

"The sacrifices and offerings on every Panegyry of Hades: on the Panegyry of the First Year; [and] the

Panegyry of the beginning of the Year: the Panegyry of the Great Year; [and] the Panegyry of the Little Year: the Panegyry of the end of the Year; [and] the Panegyry of the Great Festival: on the Panegyry of the Great Ruk-h; [and] on the Panegyry of the Little Rukh: on the Panegyry of the Five Huru of the year, [and] on the Sheteta .. sha: in the Twelfth Panegyrical Month; the Twelfth Division of the Panegyrical Month: every Panegyry of the chief of the plain-country, the good chief of the hill-country."

The second inscription is similar in character to the first; chiefly recording offerings made by a person named Nehar, or Nehra, and his father, Num-hotp, or Nev-hotp. In it we find mention of " the Panegyry of the First Year, [and that of] Thoth," of " the Great Panegyry," of the two Ruk-hs, and of the " Twelfth [Panegyrical] Month, the Twelfth Division of the [Panegyrical] Month," of "the Manifestation of Sma," of " the Sixth (?) of the Twelve Asha," of " the Five Huru of the Year," and of " the Manifestation of Sothis," &c.

With respect to the text of these inscriptions, I think it necessary here to repeat, that my copies were made with the greatest care; and to add, that I compared other copies, previously published, with the originals, and found them to be incorrect.

There is one point in my translations upon which I must here comment. I have rendered the group written with a dagger and palm-branch in the first inscription, and with a head and palm-branch in the second inscription, " the First Year." It is well known that the dagger is a sign for the ordinal " first," and it is certain that the head is used in the same manner. In the two cases before us, the ordinal precedes, instead of following, the substantive; and it has been laid down, as a general rule, that ordinal numbers, in hieroglyphics, follow the substantives to which they apply. Hence some would read this "the Beginning of the Year;" but I have found abundant evidence to show that the ordinal does sometimes precede the substantive. Further, I have found this very group written with the ordinal after the substantive, in inscriptions of the same kind as those before us, though the other form is more usual. The reason for the general deviation from common usage, in this particular case, seems to me to have been merely a desire to adopt the combination most pleasing to the eye; for in several instances we find the group "First Year" immediately preceded by the group "Beginning of the Year;" and if the group "First Year" were written in the regular manner, both the signs for "Year" would come together; but if the palm-branch is put after the dagger (as is always the case in these instances), a remarkably symmetrical group is formed.

It is evident that the two inscriptions before us record the commencement of a great period. Not only are they remarkable for containing a longer list of Panegyries than any others of a similar character that I have seen, but they make mention of two periods which I have not found mentioned on any other Egyptian monument whatever, the Great Year, and the Little Year. It is further remarkable, that the two Ruk-hs are mentioned in these inscriptions, whereas "the Ruk-h," that is, the Great Ruk-h, is alone mentioned in all the inscriptions that I have seen which record the commencement of other periods, and celebration of Panegyries, &c., with one exception. I must observe that the other periods, the records of the commencement of which have been just alluded to, are not dependent upon, nor connected with, that period of which the commencement is recorded in the Benee-Hasan inscriptions. This will be seen to be the case from what I have to say on the Calendar of the Panegyries, and from inscriptions then to be cited.

From these considerations it appears that the commencement of some very remarkable period, probably connected in some manner with the vernal equinox, or Little Ruk-h, is recorded in the Benee-Hasan inscriptions. What was the nature of this period? The monuments enable me satisfactorily to answer this question.

The persons by or for whom these inscriptions were executed lived in the reigns of Amenemha I.[1], the last King of the Eleventh Dynasty, and Sesertesen I.[2], Amenemha II.[3], and Sesertesen II.[4], the first three Kings of

the Twelfth Dynasty; but the part of the longer inscription, in which the first extract given by me occurs, relates to events which took place in the reign of Amenemha II. The approximative ancient Egyptian chronology obtained from the true order of the dynasties shows that the reign of Amenemha II. fell in the interval from B.C. 1950 to 2050. Now, within this interval the Tropical Year coincided exactly with the Vague Year. Such a coincidence could only happen at intervals of about 1500 Vague Years. The true coincidence would be in a somewhat longer period than

1500 Vague Years, but I am convinced that that is the length of the Egyptian Tropical Cycle; because, first, it is composed of a complete number of centuries; secondly, because it is nearly luni-solar; thirdly, because the Egyptians are stated by ancient writers to have had periods of 3000, and of 500 years, the double, and the third of 1500 years, respectively; and, fourthly, because we cannot suppose the ancient Egyptians to have had a more accurate Tropical Cycle than one of 1500 Vague Years. Thus we see it to be evident that the Egyptians had a Tropical Cycle consisting of 1500 Vague Years, from our finding that the coincidence of the Vague and Tropical Years which should mark the commencement of such a cycle fell in the interval which the monuments give as the approximative time of the reign of Amenemha II.

There is another evidence showing that the cycle which commenced in the reign of Amenemha II. was a Tropical Cycle, the commencement of which was marked by the coincidence of the Tropical and Vague Years. In an inscription in the British Museum, a copy of which is given in that useful work, "Sharpe's Inscriptions from the British Museum" (Pl. XVI.), we find records of offerings having been made by or for a person of the name of Hanata, surnamed Ra-num-hat-men, at the commencement of a period which I cannot but conclude to be the cycle of which I am now treating.

The title of the person by or for whom this inscription was made proves him to have been born in the reign of Amasis, the last monarch of the Twenty-sixth Dynasty; or, perhaps, during the lifetime of his son, who bore the prenomen of his father (Ra-num-hat) as his own name, and who was a person of great power, apparently a viceroy, in the reign of Darius Hystaspés.

THE TROPICAL CYCLE.

I formerly thought that this inscription was made in the time of Ra-num-hat, the supposed viceroy. This may have been the case, though this conclusion cannot be drawn from the inscription, as considered separately from the date which it records. The circumstances which I have stated limit the time at which the inscription was sculptured to some years subsequent to the year B.C. 570, the earliest date we can reasonably assign to the accession of Amasis; and in the interval that we thus obtain we find that the Vague and Tropical Years again nearly coincided, at the expiration of an interval of 1500 years after the coincidence in the time of Amenemha II.; for I have clearly shown that the Benee-Hasan inscriptions record the commencement of a Tropical Cycle with the coincidence of the Tropical and Vague Years in the reign of that King. I must now proceed to show the particular years in which this cycle commenced. It appears to me that the most appropriate name that we can apply to it is " the Tropical Cycle;" for such it was doubtless considered to be by the ancient Egyptians: I formerly called it the Ruk-h Cycle.

We cannot but conclude that the Egyptians considered the Tropical Cycle to be a perfectly exact cycle of the sun, moon, and Vague Year; and, consequently, its first year must have been marked by some coincidence of tropical and lunar phenomena on a particular day of the Vague Year. From the mention of both the Ruk-hs in the Benee-Hasan inscriptions, we might infer that the coincidence was that of the new moon and vernal equinox; and all doubt on this point is most satisfactorily removed by the fact that in the Vague Years which commenced on the day of the winter solstice or the day immediately preceding that solstice, the nearest approximation to coincidence between the new moon and winter solstice was in that year in which the new moon and vernal equinox still more nearly coincided; and the same is the case with respect to the Great Ruk-h.

Thus I have shown that the Egyptians possessed a Tropical Cycle of 1500 complete Vague Years, which was almost exactly luni-solar, and that its first year was marked by the coincidence, exact, or approximative, of the new moon and vernal equinox, or Little Ruk-h. I calculated that the new moon and vernal equinox coincided in the years B.C. 2005 and 506; but a calculation of this kind, referring to so remote a period, being extremely difficult, I applied to the Astronomer Royal, Mr. Airy, requesting that he would cause this and other similar points mentioned in the present work to be examined, and either verified or corrected, by one of his assistants at the Royal Observatory; and he not only complied with my request, but, with the greatest kindness, revised his assistants' calculations himself. Thus I find, with the utmost certainty, that the new moon of April, B.C. 2005, fell on the 8th (civil) day of that month, and the true vernal equinox fell on the preceding day, namely, the 7th; and that the new moon of March, B.C. 506, fell on the 28th day of that month, and the true vernal equinox on the preceding day, namely, the 27th. In all cases I use the civil day. For the reader's satisfaction I give Mr. Airy's calculations in an Appendix.

The Egyptian monuments, therefore, give us two fixed dates: the commencement of the first Tropical Cycle on the first day of the Tropical and Vague Years, January 7, B.C. 2005, in the reign of Amenemha II., the second King of Manetho's Twelfth Dynasty; and the commencement of the second Tropical Cycle, December 28, B.C. 507, when Egypt was a province of the Persian Empire under Darius Hystaspes.

The date of the commencement of the second Tropical Cycle is in a time well known: that of the first is in a time respecting which modern writers have very widely differed; but it is agreeable with history, sacred and profane; with the general chronology of the Egyptian monuments, and with other dates found on those monuments; and also nearly with the chronology of Champollion, followed by Rosellini. These learned authors placed the Sesertesens and Amenemhas in the Sixteenth and Seventeenth Dynasties, instead of the Eleventh and Twelfth, to which they properly belong; but they placed them so because they saw that the monuments will not allow of a considerable interval between those Kings and the Eighteenth Dynasty; and they were not aware that several of the intermediate Dynasties (between the Eleventh and the Eighteenth) were contemporary. This errour, combined with the fact of their placing the Eighteenth Dynasty too early, made them nearly correct as to the age of the Kings in question.

I must here add a few words by way of recapitulation. As I have proved beyond dispute that the two Ruk-hs designate points in the Tropical Year, a point one zodiacal month before the vernal equinox, and that equinox itself; that an Egyptian tropical cycle would consist of 1500 Vague Years; that I find indications of the commencements of such a cycle in hieroglyphic inscriptions; that one of these points to a period certainly about B.C. 507; and the other two point to a period which, according to the approximative chronology obtained from monumental and other data, to be given in Part II. of this work, is about 1500 years before the later period; and that the Tropical and Vague Years of the ancient Egyptians coincided at these two periods, as is clearly shown by natural phenomena, which are as unvarying as the courses of the planets; I think every candid reader must admit such testimony to be amply sufficient to establish the point which I have endeavoured to prove.

I have discussed the monumental records of the Tropical Cycle, and mentioned the remarkable agreement of the dates obtained from that cycle with the most venerable of ancient profane records, and the near agreement of those dates with the opinion of Champollion and Rosellini. It now only remains for me to notice, though but briefly, one confirmation of the duration which I have assigned to the Tropical Cycle, and its connection with the period of the separate state of the soul, an important point in the ancient Egyptian mythology; leaving many chronological and historical confirmations for the second part of this work, to which they more properly belong.

Herodotus[*] tells us, that the Egyptians held the doctrines of the immortality of the soul, and Metempsychosis, and believed the time of the absence of the soul from a human body to be 3000 years. Now, this is the double of a Tropical Cycle; and, accordingly, we find, upon mummy-cases and funereal tablets, representations of two sitting jackals, the emblems of the Ruk-hs. The jackal is also an emblem of the god Anubis or Ap-heru, who is represented with a jackal's head, and the latter of whose names these sitting jackals commonly bear. The signification of Anup, the Egyptian

---

[*] Herod. ii. 123.

form of Anubis, is not known; but that of Ap-heru evidently relates to the paths of the sun. Plutarch tells us that some held the opinion that Anubis was Time. At all events, it is obvious that Anubis was connected with the sun or the ecliptic, and, consequently, with the Ruk-hs; and hence it appears to me very probable that the two jackals represented on the mummy-cases, and on funereal tablets, refer to the period during which the soul was supposed to be absent from a human body.

SECTION III.

THE SOTHIC CYCLE.

THE first division of the ceiling of the Rameseum of El-Kurneh* contains representations of certain stars and asterisms, placed beneath those months of the Vague Year in which they rose heliacally, using the term in its Egyptian acceptation. The first of these representations is a boat, in which stands a female figure, shown by her name and position to be Isis-Sothis (commonly called Sothis), the Sirius of the Greeks and moderns. The head of this figure is beneath the commencement of Thoth, the first month. It is universally acknowledged that this figure and place of Sothis represent the so-called heliacal rising of that star, which was a phenomenon of the greatest importance in the ancient Egyptian calendar. It is as well known and established that the Egyptians had a great cycle of 1460 Julian and 1461 Vague Years, the commencement of which was marked by the rising of Sothis, in a certain manner, hitherto called "the heliacal rising," on the first day of the first month of the Vague Year. It is equally certain that one of these great cycles, called the "Sothic Cycles," commenced on the 20th of July, B.C. 1322; and it is generally acknowledged, having been first pointed out by the learned and accurate Sir Gardner Wilkinson, that the representation in the Rameseum of El-Kurneh dates about, or shortly

* See Plate II.

before, the commencement of that cycle which began B.C. 1322*. Since the head of the figure of Sothis is beneath the commencement of the first month, Thoth, it is evident, especially when we compare this with the other representations of the same division, that, at the time when this record was sculptured, Sothis rose in the manner which then marked the commencement of the cycle in the beginning or course of Thoth, the first month. I must now notice some remarkable particulars connected with the Sothic Cycle, which are very important in this place; not only as further explaining the ceiling of the Rameseum of El-Kurueh, but also as giving us great insight into the astronomy of the ancient Egyptians at a very early period.

It seems to have been either assumed or conceded by every one who has written on this subject, that Sothis rose heliacally at Memphis or Thebes, or at some intermediate place, on the 20th of July, B.C. 1322; but when it is suggested to the astronomer that he should not accept this assertion without testing its accuracy, a few minutes' consideration will suffice to convince him that it is untrue; although it must be admitted that, on the day above mentioned, there was a certain rising of Sothis, which marked the commencement of a Sothic Cycle. Since Sothis now rises heliacally at Memphis on or about the 20th of July, O.S., and at Thebes on or about the 17th of the same month, it is evident that in the year B.C. 1322 it must have risen heliacally some days earlier than the 20th of July. (The modern days of rising just mentioned are roughly calculated by me; assuming an arc of depression of 10°. It is probable that we should be

* Ancient Egyptians, 2nd Series, vol. i., pp. 377, 378.

justified in assuming a smaller arc of depression, considering the intense brilliancy of Sirius; but as the preceding calculations needed only to be approximative, it was not necessary to be particularly exact as to this point in this instance.) Thus the rising of Sothis on the 20th of July, B.C. 1322, which marked the commencement of the earliest known Sothic Cycle, was not what the astronomers call the heliacal rising. When I first published my opinion on this point, I said that, "according to my calculation, about twenty days after the heliacal rising of Sothis (or Sirius), that star rose at the point of the first clear indication of the morning-light at Memphis on the 20th of July, B.C. 1322." I stated this with a feeling of certainty that I was correct in the conclusion that Sothis rose some time before the time of heliacal rising on the day in question, though I expressed diffidence as to the exactness of my result, which made the rising at Memphis to be about two hours before sunrise. Hence I supposed that the phenomenon which marked the commencement of the cycle of B.C. 1322 was the rising of Sothis at the time above mentioned, and that the so-called heliacal risings of the ancient Egyptians (I mean what are so called by some writers) were phenomena of the same kind. Being in Egypt at the time when I published these observations, and having no tables by means of which I could make accurate *sidereal* calculations of this difficult nature, I was unable to arrive nearer the truth. Through the kindness of the Astronomer Royal, I can now state the correct interval from the rising of Sothis to that of the sun at the time in question; and thus I find that I have to alter my opinion on this point, though, at the same time, it is incontestably proved that I was right when I said that

Sothis did not rise heliacally either at Thebes or Memphis on the 20th of July, B.C. 1322.

The calculation made for me at the Royal Observatory gives an interval of one hour, sixteen minutes, twenty-three seconds, from the rising of Sothis to that of the sun, at Thebes, on the 20th of July, B.C. 1322. From this I find that on the same day at Memphis, Sothis rose very little more than one hour before the sun; and thus we see that the phenomenon which marked the commencement of the Sothic Cycle that began in the year B.C. 1322 was the rising of Sothis about one hour before sunrise at Memphis on the 20th of July, which then corresponded to the first day of the Vague Year.

On the monuments we find frequent mention of "the Manifestation," or "Appearance," "of Sothis;"* and this is evidently the Egyptian term for the rising which marked the commencement of the Sothic Cycle that began in the year B.C. 1322. Consequently, we may say that the actual occurrence of "the Manifestation of Sothis" on the first day of the first month of the Vague Year, or, at least, during that month, is recorded in the representations of the ceiling of the Rameseum of El-Kurueh. But Rameses III., the fourth legitimate successor of Rameses II., records, in a calendar of festivals inscribed on the great temple erected by him in western Thebes (the Rameseum of Medeenet-Haboo), that in his reign, "the Manifestation of Sothis" took place on the first day of Thoth, the first month; although, from the interval between the reigns of Rameses II. and Rameses III., it is obvious that Sothis could not have risen visibly before the sun on the first day of Thoth in the reign of the

* See Plate I., No. 7.

latter King; yet I have no doubt that the Calendar of Medeenet-Haboo is one of a Vague Year; and it appears that the Panegyry of "the Manifestation of Sothis" (the rising one hour before the sun) continued to be celebrated on the first day of Thoth as long as the phenomenon occurred in the course of that month; that is, for the space of 120 Julian years.

Hence it appears that the position of Sothis in the sculptures of the ceiling of the Rameseum of El-Kurneh shows that at the time at which those sculptures were executed the manifestation of Sothis was *celebrated* on the first day of Thoth vague; and thus we see the date of this record to be within the first hundred and twenty Julian years of the Sothic Cycle that commenced during the Nineteenth Dynasty, or from the year B.C. 1322 to 1202.

There are two important inquiries respecting the Sothic Cycle which remain to be noticed: the connection of these cycles with history, and the question as to whether there were any Sothic Cycles before that commencing in the year B.C. 1322, the earliest recorded by ancient writers of any authority.

The first known Sothic Cycle commenced on the 20th July, B.C. 1322, as already mentioned; and the second, on the same day, A.D. 139. It is well known that the latter epoch fell in the reign of the Emperor Antoninus Pius, and we find allusions to it on the coins of his reign[*]. It is the commencement of the earlier cycle, in the year B.C. 1322, which is the more important, as affording an approximative date in the chronology of Manetho's Nineteenth Dynasty, if we can satisfactorily ascertain in whose reign it took place.

[*] V. Zoega Num. Æg. referred to by Sharpe, in his valuable History of Egypt, new edition, p. 418.

MENOPHRÈS.

The well-known passage of Theon Alexandrinus, given by Cory in his "Ancient Fragments,"* speaks of the commencement of the Sothic Cycle which commenced in the year B.C. 1322 in terms which justify us in saying that it was called the Era of Menophrês. To which of the Pharaohs is this name applied? It has been suggested that ΜΕΝΟΦΡΗΣ is a corruption of some Greek transcription of the name Men-ptah, or Men-phthah. On the monuments we find four Kings bearing the name of Men-path; Men-ptah Sethee I., the father of Rameses II.; Men-ptah Hotp-har(?)-tma, the son, and Men-ptah Si-ptah, the son-in-law, of the latter King; and Men-ptah Sethee II., his second legitimate successor. I have shown that the ceiling of the Rameseum of El-Kurueh dates during the first hundred and twenty years of the Sothic Cycle which I am considering; and, consequently, the Menophrês of the Sothic Cycle would be Men-ptah Sethee I., the

father and immediate predecessor of Rameses II. This is confirmed by our finding that the earliest astronomical ceiling which has been discovered is that of the great chamber of his tomb, in which Sothis occupies a conspicuous position. The chronology of the Nineteenth Dynasty, as obtained from Manetho, shows, on being compared with the records of the risings of Sothis, that this Sothic Cycle cannot have commenced before the reign of Men-ptah Sethee I., whom Manetho calls

* Second edit., pp. 329, 330.

Sethôs, or Sethôsis. It is very remarkable that all the Kings whose names are derived from that of Seth, to whom Sothis was considered sacred, as well as to Isis, reigned, or came to the throne, during the interval in which the manifestation of Sothis was celebrated on the first day of Thoth vague. These Kings are Men-ptah Sethee I., Men-ptah Sethee II., and Seth-nekht, the father of Rameses III. Each of these Kings is likewise called after Osiris, in some instances; thus, Osiree I., Osiree II., and Osir-nekht. The mutual resemblance of the names Osiris and Sirius is here worthy of notice, more especially since relation to Isis implies relation to Osiris. In the nomen of Sir Gardner Wilkinson's Rameses VI. there is a title connected with Seth; but this title was not assumed on his coming to the throne: it was evidently given him with the name Rameses at his birth; for we find him bearing that name and title as a prince in the Rameseum of Medeenet-Haboo; and hence we cannot doubt that he was named (probably at his birth) during the interval in which the manifestation of Sothis was celebrated on the first day of Thoth. I know of no other King's name, nor of any other royal title, at all connected with Seth; and this appears to me to be a remarkable confirmation of the conclusion that the Sothic Cycle of B.C. 1322 commenced in the reign of Sethee I. We do not know, it is true, when that King was called Sethee; but it is most probable that he took that name at his accession. I cannot, however, omit to notice in this place the reason for the consecration of Sothis to Isis as well as Seth, and for the Kings being called sometimes Sethee, sometimes Osiree. The ancient Egyptians, in their mythology, according to the opinion now generally held, personified what they regarded as the beneficent power of nature, calling it Osiris and Isis; and they called what they considered the destroying power of nature, or, rather, physical evil, Seth, whom the Greeks called Typhon. Sothis was considered sacred to both powers; since, at the time of its rising, they were considered as conflicting; for the Nile then began to show the first symptoms of rising, and, at the same time, the great heat was parching up the cultivable soil.

It only remains to consider the question, whether there were any Sothic Cycles before that which commenced in the year B.C. 1322, a question of the utmost importance, and therefore deserving the most careful consideration. So many systems of Egyptian chronology have been constructed by modern writers upon the supposition that there were Sothic Cycles before the year B.C. 1322, that every one who attempts to elucidate the ancient Egyptian chronology is bound to give his reasons for adopting or rejecting this opinion. In the present, as in every other branch of this inquiry, we have two kinds of testimony to appeal to, before we give our assent or denial to the opinion in question. We must examine the statements of ancient writers, and the records upon the monuments of Egypt, and first the latter. The Egyptian monuments do not enable us to accept or deny the opinion that there were Sothic Cycles before the Era of Menophrês on direct evidence. They furnish an argument against that opinion; but it is only founded upon negative, not on affirmative, evidence. We find no direct mention whatever, as far as I know, of any Sothic Cycle upon the monuments, although we do find records of other periods, one of which is a cycle. Consequently, as we know that a Sothic Cycle did commence during the Nineteenth Dynasty, and yet find no direct mention of that cycle in the inscriptions of the time, why, it may be asked, were there no Sothic Cycles before this one, alike unmentioned on the monuments? But we do find certain indications of the Sothic Cycle which commenced in the year B.C. 1322 in the astronomical ceilings of the tombs of Sethee I. and other Kings, and in the sculptures of the ceiling of the Rameseum of El-Kurneh; and we find no similar indications in earlier periods, though older inscriptions, those of the times of the Fourth and Twelfth Dynasties, abound in mentions of periods of time. We find, moreover, that the ancient Egyptians possessed a series of chronological periods commencing in the year B.C. 2717, and that these periods were independent of any Sothic Cycles, although one of them was a cycle, similar in character and length to the Sothic. A comparison of my system of Egyptian chronology with the statements of ancient writers will be seen to show that the Egyptians had no historical chronology before the year B.C. 2717; that this date, which is less than the length of a Sothic Cycle before the Era of Menophrês, is the date of the commencement of their existence as a nation. This is, in my opinion, conclusive. The evidence of ancient writers, considered separately from what I have just mentioned, is also strongly against the opinion that there were Sothic Cycles before the Era of Menophrês. No ancient writer of the least authority, none but the impostors who composed such works as the "Book of Sothis," and the "Old Chronicle," and their followers, speak of Sothic Cycles before the year B.C. 1322; and the very name of the Era of Menophrês seems to point to a new institution, and not to the renewal of a cycle. It has been said that the reigns of the gods are composed of a certain number of Sothic Cycles; and that the Turin List of Kings, or Royal Papyrus, a record of the Nineteenth, or some subsequent Dynasty, favours this opinion. But who can base a *chronological* argument upon a *mythological* computation? Even if any hold that it is a chronological computation, to say that the Sothic Cycle is older than the Nineteenth Dynasty because the reign of the gods is reckoned by Sothic Cycles (admitting this to be the case) is just as reasonable as to say that the Julian year is as old as the creation because chronologers make use of it in computing the chronology of the world from the creation to the present time.

From the facts which I have stated, it is evident that neither the Egyptian monuments, nor ancient writers of authority, afford us any single argument in favour of the supposition that there were Sothic Cycles, or even that there was one Sothic Cycle, before that which commenced in the year B.C. 1322; but, on the contrary, give us several arguments against that supposition, one of which appears to me to be perfectly conclusive; and all of which, when considered carefully, and weighed against the want of evidence on the other side, show satisfactorily that there is no reason whatever for saying that there was even one Sothic Cycle before the year B.C. 1322.

The remark of Clemens Alexandrinus, that the Israelites went out of Egypt 345 years before the Sothic period, (γίνεται ἡ ἔξοδος κατὰ Ἴναχον πρὸ τῆς Σωθιακῆς περιόδου, ἐξελθόντος ἀπ᾽ Αἰγύπτου Μωσέως ἔτεσι πρότερον τριακοσίοις τεσσαράκοντα πέντε: "Stromata," i.,) I have not adduced in the preceding inquiry respecting the antiquity of the Sothic Cycle (although it seems decidedly in favour of my view of the case), since I admit none but arguments of the strongest kind.

SECTION IV.

THE PHŒNIX CYCLE.

I MUST now beg the reader to turn his attention again to the astronomical sculptures of the ceiling of the Rameseum of El-Kurneh*, that he may understand the bases upon which I found my identification of the Phœnix, and consequent discovery of the Phœnix Cycle. It will be necessary to examine the representations contained in the first and second divisions of the ceiling, and to decide what these representations indicate.

After the representation of Sothis, upon which I have already commented, in the first division, we find several similar representations, which I proceed to examine in regular order, that is, from right to left. We find, three times represented, under the second, third, and fourth, months, the figure of Horus in a boat, with a star above his head. As Achilles Tatius tells us that the Egyptians considered the planet Mercury sacred to Apollo (Horus), it may be supposed, as I formerly concluded, that these figures represent some phenomena of that planet; but these and other minor points, which, as far as I know, do not lend any aid to the investigations which are the subject of this work, I need not discuss.

Next to the last representation of Horus, beneath the same month, we find a constellation represented by two tortoises, and called Shetu, the situation of which, with respect to Sirius, seems to show that it

* See Plate II.

is the zodiacal constellation Libra, which would rise at this period in the same manner as Sothis rose in Thoth. That the two tortoises were a constellation in the astronomy of the ancient Egyptians is proved by our finding them represented as such in an astronomical representation on a mummy-case, copied in plate *c.* of the Bishop of Gibraltar's valuable paper on this subject*.

Continuing our examination, we are next struck by finding, beneath the sixth month, the figure of a Phœnix, accompanied by the name Ben-nu Osir†, that is, "the Phœnix of Osiris." As it is unaccompanied by any star or group of stars, it might be supposed to be strictly a chronological representation, indicating the commencement of a Phœnix period at the time at which this record was sculptured; but the astronomical representation already referred to clears up this difficulty, showing that this figure of the Phœnix represents a constellation. When I first published my opinions on Egyptian chronology, I supposed this constellation or asterism to be composed of *a* Aquilæ, and the stars in its immediate neighbourhood, judging from the interval between the rising of Sirius and that of *a* Aquilæ at the present day. I find, however, from the calculations made at the Royal Observatory, one of which gives the time of the rising of *a* Aquilæ at a period between six and seven centuries before the Era of Menophrês, that we must not limit the ancient Egyptian constellation to the stars I have mentioned. I think it most probable that the constellation of the Phœnix corresponded to Cygnus, the "Bird" (Ὄρνις)

* Transactions of the Royal Society of Literature, vol. iii., part 2.
† See Plate II.

of the Greeks, and perhaps also included Aquila, or corresponded to part of each of those constellations. Here I would particularly beg the reader to remark, that when I speak of an ancient Egyptian constellation corresponding to a constellation as laid down in our maps, I mean that they corresponded more nearly than any others, or that the one was included in the other. This constellation, therefore, rose during Mechir, the sixth month, in the same manner as Sothis rose in Thoth; that is to say, its principal, or last, star so rose.

Proceeding with the examination of this division of the ceiling, we find, under the ninth month, a representation of the Boat of the Sun; and under the tenth month, a representation of a ram or sheep. It is remarkable that these occupy the places which correspond to a supposed constellation containing the star called Markab, مركب, that is, the "Ship" or "Boat," in Arabic; and to Aries; if we infer that they are represented as rising, in the same manner as Sothis did in the first month, in the months under which they are placed; and this I formerly believed to be the case; but I am now convinced that they belong to the Calendar of the Decans, which will be the subject of the next section. The same is the case with two other representations in this part of the first division.

The second division has, like the others, several vertical subdivisions, the central of which nearly corresponds to Mesori and the Epagomenæ, and contains representations of six constellations or asterisms, which rose during this portion of the year in the same manner as Sothis did in Thoth. Among these are the Bull, with the hieroglyphic name Mes-ra, undoubtedly the zodiacal constellation Taurus; and a hawk-headed figure which I cannot doubt to be Orion. Plutarch tells us that Orion was the constellation of Horus, who is one of the gods whom we find represented on the monuments with a hawk's head.

I have shown in the preceding remarks, that an asterism or constellation partly or wholly corresponding to Cygnus, and, perhaps, also to Aquila, is represented in the sculptures of the ceiling of the Rameseum of El-Kurneh by the Phœnix, called in hieroglyphics "the Phœnix of Osiris," Bennu Osir. There can be no doubt that the Bennu is the Phœnix. The figure of a bird with human hands*, which some have supposed to represent the Phœnix, is known from its name, Rekheet, properly to signify "a pure soul." This, indeed, is shown also to emblematize some period or cycle, by a passage in the hieroglyphic inscriptions of the Sarcophagus of Queen Ankh-nes, in the British Museum, which speaks of "the period of pure souls."† It, however, evidently does not refer to the true Phœnix Cycle, but to the cycle of the separate state of the soul, which I have already shown to have been probably a longer period than what I shall prove the Phœnix Cycle to be. The Phœnix is historical; but the other period, merely mythical, and not commencing from any one fixed date, but from the time of each person's death, according to the mythology of the ancient Egyptians. Still, as the period of the separate state of the soul was emblematized by a bird, generally represented with a partly human form, but sometimes by a simple bird, it is very easy to see that it may have been confounded, in late times, with the Phœnix Cycle.

* See Plate I., Nos. 8 and 9.   † Ibid., No. 9.

I have shown what the Phœnix was in the astronomy of the ancient Egyptians. Ancient writers tell us of the appearance of the Phœnix at various times: this must have been the appearance of the constellation, or of its most remarkable star; and, as the rising of Sothis about one hour before sunrise is what is meant, in hieroglyphics, by the expression, "the appearance" or "manifestation" of that star, the appearance of the Phœnix was evidently the rising of that constellation, that is, of its principal, or of its last, star, at the same time before sunrise. But the commencement of the first Sothic Cycle was marked by the rising of Sothis about one hour before sunrise on the first day of the Vague Year; and, consequently, we might conclude that the Phœnix Cycle commenced when some particular star of that ancient Egyptian constellation rose at the same time on the first day of the Vague Year. I shall be able to show, in a subsequent place (Sect. 6), that a subdivision of a cycle exactly similar to the Phœnix had been previously instituted; and a commencement of a cycle beginning with one of those subdivisions was called the appearance of the Phœnix, from the circumstance that "the manifestation" of a principal star of that constellation at that time fell in the first month of the Vague Year, and was celebrated, according to Egyptian usage, on the first day of that month. Now, since the commencement of each Phœnix Cycle was marked by the occurrence or celebration of the phenomenon just mentioned on a particular day of the Vague Year, it is obvious that the Phœnix Cycle was composed of about 1460 Julian, or 1461 Vague Years, like the Sothic, being as correct a cycle of that nature as the Egyptians could form from observation; and from these considerations, we see that the representations of the ceiling of the Rameseum fix the commencement of a Phœnix Cycle to some one of the years B.C. 2042 to 1923 inclusive, and give an idea of its length. This is too obvious to demand explanation.

Tacitus, speaking of the Phœnix, in a well-known passage, says, " Concerning the number of years there are various accounts: the most common period is 500: some assert that the interval is 1461; and that former birds flew to the city called Heliopolis, accompanied by many other fowls which were astonished at the strange appearance, first in the reign of Sesostris, afterwards in that of Amasis, and then in that of Ptolemy, who was the third Macedonian sovereign." (De numero annorum varia traduntur. Maxime vulgatum quingentorum spatium; sunt qui adseverent mille quadringentos sexaginta unum interjici. Prioresque alites Sesostride primum, post Amaside, dominantibus; dein Ptolemæo, qui ex Macedonibus tertius regnavit, in civitatem, cui Heliopolis nomen, advolavisse, multo ceterarum volucrum comitatu, novam faciem mirantium*.)

This statement enables us to obtain nearer approximative dates of two appearances of the Phœnix; for the reign of Amasis lasted from the year B.C. 570 to 525, at most, and this falls within the approximative extremes obtained from the representations of the ceiling of the Rameseum. But before proceeding in this investigation, I must remark that the smaller periods, with one of which the Phœnix commenced, show that the duration of that period was 1461 Julian years, not 1460. This would make the cycle slightly inaccurate, so that, after 5844 years, there would be an errour of a

* An. vi. 28.

day in the coincidence of the Vague and Julian Years. The prospect of this errour, however, is not likely to have been regarded by the originators of the Egyptian system. Assuming this duration of 1461 years to be correct, and I shall soon be able to state my reasons for believing in its correctness, we obtain approximations to the dates of the first two appearances of the Phœnix mentioned by Tacitus much nearer than those obtained from the ceiling of the Rameseum of El-Kurneh; namely, some time in the reign of Amasis, B.C. 570 to 525, the appearance of the Phœnix of Amasis; and 1461 Julian years earlier, B.C. 2031 to 1986, the appearance of the Phœnix of Sesôstris; and this latter date agrees with my approximative chronology of the Twelfth Dynasty, previously obtained from the commencement of the Tropical Cycle in the reign of Amenemha II. The Phœnix of the third Macedonian King, as Tacitus terms one of the Ptolemies, I shall have to notice in a future page.

Before I discovered the true Phœnix Cycle, I had concluded that the ancient Egyptians made use of a chronological period of 365 Julian years, to which I gave the appellation of the Great Panegyrical Year, and that four of those periods composed a cycle of 1460 Julian years. I calculated, also, that two of those periods of 365 Julian years commenced B.C. 1985-4 and 525-4. Since publishing that opinion, I have been induced, by a change in my views respecting the length of a small subdivision of the Great Panegyrical Year (to be explained when I come to treat of that period), to determine its mean length to be $365\frac{1}{4}$ Julian years, and the dates of commencements which I have just mentioned to be January 2nd, B.C. 1986, and the same day B.C. 525. Since both fall within the approximative limits of the commencements of two Phœnix Cycles, I conclude that these two dates of the commencements of Great Panegyrical Years are likewise the dates of the appearances of the Phœnixes of Sesôstris and Amasis, and that the Great Panegyrical Year commencing in the year B.C. 1986, and each following one, began with a quarter of a Phœnix Cycle. It is evident that a cycle commencing with that Great Panegyrical Year which began in the year B.C. 1986 was called a Phœnix Cycle, because at its commencement the manifestation of the Phœnix was celebrated on the first day of Thoth. Thus we obtain the true dates of the appearances of the Phœnix; first, approximatively, from the astronomical sculptures of the ceiling of the Rameseum of El-Kurueh; then, more nearly, but still approximatively, from the remarkable record, perhaps derived from Manetho, transmitted to us by Tacitus; and then, at last, truly and accurately, from the commencements of Panegyrical periods, fixed by means of the recorded dates on the ancient Egyptian monuments. No one of these steps in the process of fixing the commencement of the most perplexing of ancient periods is in any way dependent on another: all are independent, separate, and possessed of high authority. It is to be remembered, also, that when I wrote on the Great Panegyrical Year, I had not formed even a guess, much less an opinion, as to the length and character of the Phœnix Cycle; so that I had in fact already determined it, before I was aware of there being any record of it upon the ancient Egyptian monuments. It is also to be remembered, that the Great Panegyrical Year was not a subdivision of the Phœnix Cycle before the appearance of the Phœnix of Sesôstris. Any one who will consider these things will be convinced that the Phœnix, that mythic bird, respecting which the learned have been at variance from the times of the Greeks and Romans to the present day, is at length identified, and that the period of its appearance is ascertained, so that it can be no longer said that the most interesting of the Egyptian cycles is only explained by conjecture. Its importance to chronology and history is very great: from it we find who was the Sesôstris of the Phœnix, and obtain another date, besides that of the commencement of the Tropical Cycle, in the remote age of the Twelfth Dynasty.

It would be interesting could we ascertain what is the star with the manifestation of which the Phœnix Cycles commenced; but it is to be feared that this cannot as yet be satisfactorily ascertained. I speak of the manifestation of the star for brevity's sake in this place, meaning, as must be evident from what I have already said, either the manifestation or the celebration of that phenomenon. When I first published on Egyptian chronology, I concluded that the commencement of the Phœnix Cycle was marked by "the rising of a Aquilæ at the time of the first clear indication of the morning-light on the first day of the vague Thoth." I was, however, in errour as to the time before sunrise at which a Aquilæ rose at the commencement of the first Phœnix Cycle; for one of the calculations made for me at the Royal Observatory, through Mr. Airy's kindness, and verified by him, gives the rising of a Aquilæ on January 2nd, B.C. 1985, as two hours, seventeen minutes, forty-five seconds, before the sun, at Thebes. This calculation was made for the first date that I assigned to the commencement of the first Phœnix Cycle. I now have ascertained the date to be one year earlier; but the difference in this case is not material. Hence we see that the year B.C. 1986 was within the period of 120 years, during which the manifestation of α Aquilæ may have been celebrated on the first day of Thoth; and it is not improbable, from its being the most remarkable star in what probably composed the constellation called by the Egyptians the Phœnix, that it was the star which marked the commencement of the Phœnix periods.

Before noticing briefly the other statements respecting the Phœnix, to be found in the works of ancient writers, I must make some remarks upon the King in whose reign the first appearance of the Phœnix happened, namely, Sesôstris. As I have shown the date of this occurrence to have been in the year B.C. 1986, it is evident that the King is the Sesôstris of Manetho, the third King of Manetho's Twelfth Dynasty, and not the Sesôstris of Herodotus, the second King of Manetho's Nineteenth Dynasty. We must now endeavour to ascertain to what King mentioned in the hieroglyphic inscriptions the Sesôstris of Manetho corresponds. In the list called the Tablet of Abydos, Sesertesen II. corresponds to Manetho's Sesôstris; but in the list of the Chamber of Kings, two erased names occur in the places of Sesertesen II. and III., and Amenemha III.; and, consequently, we cannot say whether in this list Sesertesen II. or III. occupies the place of Manetho's Sesôstris. But what Manetho says respecting his Sesôstris plainly shows him to be Sesertesen III.

After having given a short account of the conquests of

THE SESOSTRIS OF MANETHO.

Sesôstris, the historian tells us that he was considered by the Egyptians as the first after Osiris. The only true explanation of this passage is, that this King was considered by the Egyptians as the greatest of mortals, and to be honoured next after Osiris, "the youngest of the gods." This explanation is most strikingly confirmed by a fact of which very remarkable instances are found in some of the unpublished papers of Sir Gardner Wilkinson, which he has kindly shown me, as well as in his published works; that in numerous sculptures in Nubia we find Kings of the Eighteenth Dynasty, of the Thothmes family, worshipping Sesertesen III. as a god, and that this is *the only case* of the kind; for although we find one solitary case of another early monarch being worshipped, and some cases of several monarchs being worshipped together, and several cases of Kings worshipping their fathers or other progenitors, yet, as far as I know, we never find another instance of a King of any dynasty being frequently represented as a god, and worshipped, in sculptures of other Kings not of the same dynasty*. On these grounds, I cannot hesitate for a moment to decide that Sesertesen III. is the Sesôstris of Manetho. A question here arises, however, since it is evident from this that Sesertesen is the Egyptian name which the Greeks write Sesôstris. Is each of the three Sesertesens a Sesôstris? We may, indeed, reasonably suppose that this similarity of name has caused some confusion; and there seems to be scarcely any doubt that two of the Sesertesens have been celebrated under the name of Sesôstris. If we

* The lists of Kings in the second part of this work, and my reasons for their arrangement, will explain any difficulties which may occur to the reader with reference to the order of the different Kings and dynasties.

were to consider which of the three Kings was the Sesôstris famous for his conquests, we should at once say Sesertesen I., who appears undoubtedly to have been the most powerful monarch of his dynasty. It seems to me that Sesertesen I. is Sesôstris the conqueror, and Sesertesen III. Sesôstris the lawgiver, though I see no reason for supposing that the latter King did not distinguish himself by foreign conquests. Some may object to this explanation, that the Egyptians could not have had a great conqueror among their Kings while the Shepherds were in Egypt. This is an erroneous supposition: the Shepherd-Kings of the Fifteenth Dynasty were merely contemporary Kings ruling in Lower Egypt, and in the time of Sesertesen I. most probably at peace with the Egyptians, and probably the Egyptians were aided by them. The whole history of the Pharaohs shows that they had often foreign troops; mercenaries, or allies, or both.

In accordance with what Tacitus remarks, we find that the most common period assigned to the return of the Phœnix, by ancient writers, was 500 years; and Herodotus, among the Greeks, and Horapollo, among the Egyptians, with many others, speak of the same period of 500 years. I think it most probable that this is "the Little Year" mentioned in the longer Benee-Hasan inscription. Since it is there mentioned immediately after "the Great Year," it appears to have been connected with that period, which I have shown to be the Tropical Cycle of 1500 Vague Years, and to have commenced with it. Its most probable length would be 500 years, which would, if composed of Vague Years, exactly correspond to one-third of the Tropical Cycle, and be the period in which the Vague Year retrograded through one season of the Tropical Year, according to the Egyptians. It is possible, however, that the Little Year may be the Twenty-five-year Cycle, also mentioned by ancient writers, which was almost a perfect cycle of lunations and Vague Years. It is necessary here to remark, that the Phœnix was supposed by Greek and Roman writers, and even by some of the Egyptians themselves, in late times, that is, during the Roman domination, and perhaps the Greek, to return at periods which had no connection whatever with the true Phœnix Cycle. The difficulties produced by this confusion are removed by the discovery of the true period.

The modern Persians and Arabs relate many marvellous things concerning a gigantic bird or birds which they call the "Rukh'," رُخ, "'Anka," عنقاء, and "Seemurgh," سيمرغ. El-Kazweenee gives an account of the 'Anka, which resembles the well-known fable of the Phœnix. My uncle (Mr. E. W. Lane) has noticed this account in the notes of his "Translation of the Thousand and One Nights,"* remarking on the similarity of the two fables. El-Kazweenee states the period of the life of the 'Anka to be 1700 years. It is very remarkable that the cycle of the separate state of the soul was supposed to be a period of twice the length of the Tropical Cycle, and was apparently emblematized by two jackals, the emblems of Anubis and the Ruk-hs, and was also emblematized certainly by a *bird*, called Rekheet, or "the pure soul," its name being "the period of pure souls." The similarity of "Rekheet" and "Ruk-h" to "Rukh'" is very striking, since the radicals of all three names are the same,

* Vol. iii. p. 91.

excepting that the k and h of the Egyptian "Ruk-h" occur in the place of the kh' of the Arabic "Rukh'" (the accent indicates reduplication): in Rekheet, the final t is augmentative. This suggests a curious inquiry respecting the origin of the connection between the two fables, and the extent to which the Persians and Arabs may have borrowed from the Egyptians and Greeks.

SECTION V.

THE CALENDAR OF THE DECANS.

THE ancient Egyptians had a calendar which we may call that of the Decans. They distinguished thirty-six stars or asterisms, nearly equidistant, throughout a great circle of the heavens (like the signs of the Zodiac), which rose at intervals of about ten days. Perhaps they regulated their agricultural and other pursuits by this calendar, just as the Arabs did in ancient times by means of their similar calendar of the Mansions of the Moon, منازل القمر, which were twenty-eight in number, corresponding to the mean daily stages of the moon; a kind of calendar which was also used by many other nations. In the ceiling of the Rameseum of El-Kurneh, we find all the Decans, excepting Sothis, crowded into the last six months and the Epagomenæ; and unequal numbers are placed beneath the several months; whence we plainly see that nothing but the position of Sothis and the order of the Decans is regarded in this instance. It is necessary to add, that in this portion of the ceiling of the Rameseum, certain constellations, to which I have already alluded, are represented among the Decans: these are evidently representations of remarkable constellations, containing certain Decans, of which the names accompany them.

It would be a work of great difficulty, to say the least, and one which would not in the least degree aid the inquiries which I am prosecuting in this volume, to point out the particular stars or asterisms of which this calendar is composed. The indications are too insufficient to guide us in such an investigation; and if we calculated the true places of a multitude of stars, and found those which agreed in the times of rising with the several Decans, in the age to which any one of the lists of the Decans belongs, we should still be bewildered in the choice.

This short account of the Calendar of the Decans is a necessary introduction to the subject of the section here immediately following.

SECTION VI.

THE CALENDAR OF THE PANEGYRIES.

ON innumerable ancient Egyptian monuments of all times, from the tombs of the age of the Fourth Dynasty at Memphis, to the temples of the Ptolemaic and Roman periods, we find mention of religious festivals, commonly called, by writers on Egyptian archæology, Panegyries. The hieroglyphic name reads Heb*. Different signs were employed as symbols of different kinds of Panegyries; but the name I have just mentioned was the general name of the ancient Egyptian religious festivals. The Greek text of the Rosetta-stone translates Heb by Panegyry, Πανήγυρις.

A period denoted by the characters in Plate III., Nos. 1, 2, 3, and 4, I call "the Great Panegyrical Month," or, by way of abbreviation, "G. P. M." The first form reads "Sidereal Month," or simply "Month;" the second and third have the same signification, with the addition of "Panegyrical;" and the fourth reads, "Sidereal and Solar Month (or Month only) of the solar Panegyry." It must be remarked that the signification of the hand, in two of these groups, is not certain; but this does not affect the general signification.

An Egyptian civil month is- a period containing thirty subdivisions, viz., days; therefore, a period con-

* Plate III., Nos. 15, 16.

taining thirty Julian years might be called by the Egyptians, who supposed those years to be solar, a Great Month, agreeably with analogy. A further argument for assigning this duration to the G. P. M. is derived from a fact which we learn from the monuments, that a subdivision of it had a minimum length of a year and a half, and that at least fifteen of these subdivisions were contained in it. Thus the monuments show us, that the G. P. M. must have contained at least twenty-two years and a half, which is so near the duration that analogy would induce us to assign to it, that we cannot hesitate to accept the latter.

A period denoted by the characters given in Plate III., Nos. 5, 6, 7, 8, 9, I call "the Division of the Great Panegyrical Month," or, abbreviated, "the Division of the G. P. M." The literal meaning of the groups which I have given is, "Division of the Sidereal Month," or "of the Month" in the instances of the first and second forms; and the same, with the addition of "Panegyrical," in the instances of the third and fourth forms; and "of the Solar Panegyry" in the fifth form. The hand, which I have already shown to have a doubtful signification in cases of this kind, though it cannot alter the general signification of the group, occurs in the fourth form. I have found dates of the Twelfth Division of the Twelfth G. P. M., and of the Fifteenth Division of the Sixth G. P. M. This convinces me that the Division of the G. P. M. had not a longer duration than two Julian years, for the length of the G. P. M. cannot be supposed to be more than thirty years.

The Calendar of the Decans affords us the means of accurately determining the length of the Division of the Great Panegyrical Month. The nineteenth Decan, counting Sothis as the first, is called "Smat, the star of the Division of the G. P. M.,"* in the sculptures of the ceiling of the Rameseum of El-Kurneh; and, being the nineteenth, it is 180°, or half a year, distant from Sothis. It is evident, therefore, that the nineteenth Decan, reckoning Sothis as the first, in the time of Rameses II. had a connection with the Division of the G. P. M.; and from this remarkable fact we cannot but infer that, in the time of that King, the commencement of the Division of the G. P. M. was sometimes marked by the rising of the nineteenth Decan. Now, the Decan of the First Division of the G. P. M. must have been the Decan of the G. P. M., that is, the Decan at, or about, the rising of which the G. P. M. commenced. But the monuments clearly show that the G. P. M. commenced in the time of Rameses II. at, or about, the time of the rising of Sothis. Therefore, the Division of the G. P. M. then commenced sometimes at the rising of Sothis, and sometimes at the rising of the nineteenth Decan. From this we must infer its length to have been half a year, or a year and a half, or some number of whole years and a half, since we thus find that it must have commenced alternately at opposite points of the year; but I have previously shown that its length did not exceed two years, and, therefore, it could only have been half a year, or a year and a half. That the latter is the true length is shown by our finding records of the first year of a G. P. M. and of a Division of the G. P. M. in the hieroglyphic inscriptions; and besides this, all probability is in

* See Plate III., No. 11.

favour of this duration, which is exactly the half of the Three-year period of Royal Panegyries, to be noticed in the next section. Thus we see that what I call the Division of the Great Panegyrical Month was the twentieth part of the Great Panegyrical Month, and had a length of one Julian year and a half.

In this place it is necessary to remove some difficulties, and to show the incorrectness of certain explanations of the Panegyrical periods. It is to be observed that the simplest characters denoting the G. P. M. were sometimes used, perhaps as early as the Nineteenth Dynasty, for an ordinary month; but, from the time of the Eighteenth Dynasty downwards, we find the more complete groups made use of, almost invariably, to denote the G. P. M. and its Division, to prevent mistake.

There are two ways in which it has been proposed to explain the G. P. M. and the Division of the G. P. M. The first hypothesis is, that the G. P. M. was a common month or a lunation, and that the Division of the G. P. M. was a half-month or half-lunation. This is disproved by our finding dates of the Fifteenth Division of the Sixth G. P. M., and of the Twelfth Division of the Twelfth G. P. M., and by the Decan of the Division of the G. P. M. If these be read sixth month, fifteenth half-month, &c., the hypothesis is equally untenable. The second hypothesis is, that the G. P. M. was a common month or lunation, and the Division of the G. P. M. a period of the same duration commencing in the middle of the former. The dates just mentioned equally disprove this.

The highest date which I have found of the G. P. M.'s is of the Twelfth; and this shows that the length of the period which they composed could not be less than 360 years. This and analogy led me to the conclusion that the ancient Egyptians had a Great Panegyrical Year of 365 Tropical Years, containing twelve Great Panegyrical Months, and five intercalary years, corresponding to the five Epagomenæ of the Vague Year. For Tropical I now say Julian, being convinced that the Egyptians believed the Julian to be a tropical and sidereal year at the early period when their calendar was instituted. The connection of the G. P. M. and its Division with Sothis and Smat plainly shows that those periods were composed of Julian years.

Having thus obtained the exact lengths of the G. P. M. and the Division of the G. P. M., and an approximative length of the Great Panegyrical Year, or G. P. Y., I next apply these results to the chronology as derived from the monuments, but derived without the help of dates, as will be seen in Part II. of this work; and, examining certain dates of Panegyrical periods on the monuments, I find the space from the first to the second, from the second to the third, and from the third to the fourth, as agreeable with the approximative chronology derived from the monuments as could be expected.

But in making this application I find certain striking peculiarities, which greatly assist me in fixing the exact length of the G. P. Y. These peculiarities indicate that the first G. P. Y. probably commenced with the manifestation of Sothis; that the second did commence with that of Smat; that the third probably commenced with that of Smat; that the fourth did commence with that of Sothis; that the fifth did also commence with that of Sothis; that the sixth probably commenced with that of Smat; and that the seventh did commence with that of Smat. Thus I obtain the following order of commencements of successive G. P. Y.'s.

1 with the manifestation of Sothis.
$\left.\begin{array}{r}2\\3\end{array}\right\}$ . . . . Smat.
$\left.\begin{array}{r}4\\5\end{array}\right\}$ . . . . Sothis.
$\left.\begin{array}{r}6\\7\end{array}\right\}$ . . . . Smat.

The custom of the ancient Egyptians in chronology was to stop short, rather than to exceed, when they were obliged to do either the one or the other, as we see (for example) in the case of the Vague Year and its divisions. The necessity of their doing so in the present instance is also shown by the Division of the G. P. M.; for it was obviously desirable that each G. P. Y. should consist of an exact number of these periods. Therefore it was most natural that they should make their G. P. Y. to consist alternately of $364\frac{1}{2}$ and 366 Julian years, and the first G. P. Y. to be of the former length. This mode of division would make the mean length of the G. P. Y. to be $365\frac{1}{4}$ Julian years, and would fulfil all the conditions required by the several data upon which this inquiry is based.

We see, therefore, that the Great Panegyrical Year was alternately $364\frac{1}{2}$ and 366 Julian years in length, thus having a mean length of $365\frac{1}{4}$ Julian years, and being evidently regarded by the Egyptians as strictly analogous to the Julian Year, which contained $365\frac{1}{4}$ solar periods; and that it commenced with the manifestation of either Sothis or Smat; that the Great Panegyrical Month contained thirty Julian years, and commenced with the manifestation of the Decan of the G. P. Y.*; and that the Division of the Great Panegyrical Month contained one Julian year and a half, and commenced alternately with the manifestation of the Decan of the G. P. M., and that of the opposite Decan. It now remains to apply this explanation of the periods of Panegyries to dates found upon the monuments.

The first date which I have found accompanied by a King's name is in a tomb in that part of the great Memphite burial-ground which is adjacent to the Great Pyramid and to the Second Pyramid. This date I give in Plate III., No. 12, omitting the usual mention of offerings which precedes it.

I have already, in speaking of the Tropical Cycle (Sect. 2), had occasion to prove that the dagger and palm-branch signify " First Year;" and I gave what I think to be the reason for the deviation from general usage in the disposition of these characters. The same is the case with two other groups in this passage, which I read " First G. P. M.," and " First Division of the G. P. M.," the interpretation of which is quite certain.

The inscription which I am now considering relates that a certain person made offerings in the commencement of the First Year of the First G. P. M., and the First Division of the G. P. M.; that is, in the commencement of a Great Panegyrical Year; and that he lived in the time of King Num-Shufu. In a similar inscription, on the outside of the tomb, evidently re-

---

* For an example of the mention of the Decan of the G. P. M. see Plate III., No. 10, " The G. P. M. (of) Smat," from an inscription in a tomb near the Pyramids of El-Geezeh.

cording the same date, but much injured, we find mention of King Shufu. These names are written in hieroglyphics Num-shufu, or Num-khufu[1], and Shufu or Khufu[2]. In each case I prefer reading the sieve " sh," since

Manetho transcribes each name by Sûphis, (Σοῦφις,) though this character generally has the value of " kh." These two royal names are evidently those of the two Sûphises of Manetho, the second and third Kings of the Fourth Dynasty, according to the version of Africanus; Shufu being the first Sûphis. I formerly supposed the two names to apply to one King, but now it is my opinion that they are the names of the two Kings just mentioned, whom I believe to have reigned together. My reasons for these conclusions will be fully stated in the second part of this work.

Having ascertained that a Great Panegyrical Year commenced in the reign of the two Sûphises, I have now to show what particular Great Panegyrical Year this was. The basis of the calculations for ascertaining the dates of the commencements of G. P. Y.'s is the date of the commencement of the Tropical Cycle in the reign of Amenemha II., B.C. 2005, in the course of the Twelfth Division of the Twelfth G. P. M. From this I find the commencement of that G. P. Y. in which the date last mentioned fell to have been in the year B.C. 2352, and the commencement of the preceding one B.C. 2717. That the G. P. Y. which began B.C. 2352 is that of

Sect. VI.] ERA OF MENES. 63

the time of the two Sûphises, I shall show in Part II., from the approximative chronology of the interval from the Sûphises to Amenemha II., derived from Manetho and the monuments.

The commencement of the Great Panegyrical Year which preceded that of the Sûphises I have already shown to be in the year B.C. 2717. That this was the First G. P. Y. is proved by the characteristics which it possesses; for it commenced in a year in which the manifestation of Sothis fell in the first month of the Vague Year, and was therefore celebrated on the first day of that month. Further, if we made another such period to have preceded this, we should refer its commencement to an age far anterior to any indicated by the monuments; for the interval from the accession of Mênês (the first King of Egypt) to the Sûphises is undoubtedly very much less than two G. P. Y.s; and I shall be able to show, in Part II., that the date of the year B.C. 2717 is the Era of the commencement of the Egyptian race, and that of Mênês.

The date of the commencement of the First Great Panegyrical Year, B.C. 2717, and that of the Second, B.C. 2352, the first being the Era of Mênês, and the second in the time of the two Sûphises, will be seen to be perfectly agreeable with the records on the Egyptian monuments.

The next date after that of the time of the Sûphises is that of the commencement of the Tropical Cycle, in the reign of Amenemha II., the second King of the Twelfth Dynasty, in the year B.C. 2005.

In treating of the Phœnix Cycle (Section IV.), I have shown that the First Phœnix Cycle commenced with the Third Great Panegyrical Year, B.C. 1986, in the reign of Sesertesen III., whom Manetho makes the third King of the Twelfth Dynasty. This, like the preceding date, has already been fully noticed.

I have not found any date recorded on the monuments from the time of the Twelfth Dynasty to that of the Eighteenth. I have, however, found three dates of the time of the latter Dynasty. The first of these is of the reign of a King of the time of the early part of the Eighteenth Dynasty, who is not found in the lists of Manetho, nor in those of the monuments, and therefore was not a legitimate sovereign. His name is read by Champollion " Skhaï;" but several other readings have

been proposed, and most hieroglyphic scholars are undecided as to the true reading. The time of his reign has likewise been considered as doubtful. Sir Gardner Wilkinson has pointed out, in his "Materia Hieroglyphica," that he was anterior to Rameses II., the second King of the Nineteenth Dynasty; and it has been generally concluded that he was anterior to Horus, the ninth King of the Eighteenth Dynasty. The application of this date to the lists shows us (as will be seen in Part II.) that Skhaï, or Skhee, was contemporary with Thothmes I., the third King of the Eighteenth Dynasty; for although he appears to have ruled at Thebes, since his tomb is there, we cannot suppose that he was not contemporary with some King found in the lists of Manetho, and those of the monuments. The inscription which contains the date I have now to notice is copied in Plate 106 of Sharpe's "Inscriptions:" it records that the fourth year of a King whose name is erased, but whose square title remains, dated in the First Division of the Sixth G. P. M. This King is Skhee; for Mr. Birch, of the British Museum, a scholar well known for his extensive and accurate knowledge of Egyptian archæology, assures me that the square title is a variation of that usually found with his name. The First Division of the Sixth G. P. M. commenced in July, B.C. 1472; and the succeeding Division commenced in January, B.C. 1470. This gives the date of Skhee's fourth year, 1472-1, and shows that he came to the throne in some part of the years B.C. 1475-4.

The next date which I have found I believe to be of the time of Queen Amen-numt, who reigned for a

time conjointly with Thothmes II. and Thothmes III. The date is in a tomb at Thebes, where the royal name has been almost entirely obliterated by the wantonness of travellers, or the deliberate plunder of those who should have set a better example. From the style of its paintings, the tomb evidently belongs to the earlier part of the Eighteenth Dynasty, and what remains of the royal name shows that it was painted in the time of Amenoph I., II., or III., or Queen Amen-numt. I formerly stated that my uncle, Mr. E. W. Lane, was almost certain that he remembered this tomb to be of the time of Amenoph II., and thought it highly probable that, when he examined it some years ago, the King's name was uninjured. Since I published this opinion, my uncle has found among his papers a note

F

which shows that the name was so far erased when he saw it that he could not say to which of the monarchs I have mentioned it applied. The mention of offerings having been made in a particular Division of a Great Panegyrical Month, which the next date that I have to notice proves to have fallen in the reign of Queen Amen-numt, merely shows that the principal person buried in this tomb lived during her reign; though, at the same time, there is no sound reason for concluding that he did not live many years more after the conclusion of that reign. I give a copy of the date in Plate III., No. 13.

This inscription refers to the celebration of certain Panegyries in the Sixth G. P. M. and the Fifteenth Division of the G. P. M. The date is, therefore, of the year B.C. 1451, or 1450; for the Fifteenth Division of the Sixth G. P. M. of the Fourth G. P. Y. commenced in July B.C. 1451, and the next Division commenced in January, B.C. 1449. The inscription is of very great importance, as mentioning such a high number of the Divisions of the G. P. M. as the Fifteenth. The Panegyries noticed in it are those of the "Waka," respecting which I have not formed a certain opinion; the Panegyry of Thoth, "the great Manifestation, the Manifestation of Sothis," and the Panegyries of the Great and Little Ruk-hs.

Another date, only a few years later than the last which I have mentioned, is found in an inscription on the base of the great obelisk of El-Karnak, a copy of which is given by M. Prisse, in Plate XVIII. of his supplement to Champollion's "Monumens de l'Égypte et de la Nubie." From it we learn that the Seventh G. P. M. commenced in Mesori of the sixteenth year of Queen Amen-numt. The date of the commencement of this G. P. M. is

July, B.C. 1442, which shows that the Queen came to the throne in the Vague Year corresponding to B.C. 1458-7. The reason of this ambiguity with respect to the Julian Year of this sovereign's accession is because we are not aware how early she began to reign in that Vague Year which was called, according to the ancient Egyptian custom, her first year, and which commenced in the Julian Year B.C. 1458, and concluded in 1457.

I have found no more mention of the Periods of Panegyries until the time of the Twenty-sixth Dynasty. In the celebrated tomb of Fa-bak-en-renf, a high functionary of the time of Psammetichus II., we find a date of this time. This tomb, which is at Memphis, is celebrated for containing one of the oldest instances of the stone arch. I conclude that the date is during the reign of Psammetichus II., since no other King is mentioned in this large tomb, and since it is merely the date of the commencement of a G. P. M. without the number being specified. This must have been the G. P. M. which commenced B.C. 591, in the reign of Psammetichus II. I obtain the chronology of this part of the Twenty-sixth Dynasty from a comparison of the well-known inscription on a stela in the museum of Florence, which reckons seventy-one years from the third year of Neco (the Nechaô II. of Manetho) to the thirty-fifth of Amasis, with what Manetho and Herodotus say respecting the lengths of the Kings' reigns.

Another date of the time of the Twenty-sixth Dynasty is of the commencement of a G. P. M. in the time of Amasis; for although that King's prenomen alone occurs in the inscription containing the date*, and that prenomen is also the name of his son, who was a high

* Transactions of the Royal Society of Literature, Vol. i. Part I., Pl. LXII.

functionary under Darius Hystaspes, yet in this case we see that it must be the King's prenomen, from the royal title which accompanies it. This date can only be that of the commencement of the G. P. M. which immediately followed that of the time of Psammetichus II., and began in the year B.C. 561.

One more date recorded on the monuments remains to be mentioned: it is of the commencement of a G. P. M. and a Division of a G. P. M. The inscription which records it is found in the largest tomb at Thebes, that of Pet-amen-apt. It is remarkable that no name of a known King occurs in this tomb, but only the name of an unplaced King or viceroy, not elsewhere found. This name is mentioned in Sir Gardner Wilkinson's "Modern Egypt and Thebes."* I was unable to find it during my last visit to Thebes, owing to its occurring but once, and to the great extent of the tomb; and I have to thank Sir Gardner for his kindness in giving me a copy of it, which I here insert. It reads Hor-em-

heb, and resembles the nomen of King Horus of the Eighteenth Dynasty, which reads "Men-amen Hor-em-heb;" and from this it might be supposed to be a

variation of that nomen. This supposition is, however,

* Vol. ii., p. 222.

inadmissible (unless Hor-em-heb is not spoken of as a King of that time, which the mutilated state of the inscription in which his name occurs does not enable us to decide); for the style of the tomb is undoubtedly that of the latter part of the Twenty-sixth Dynasty, and, perhaps, also of the Twenty-seventh. The name Hor-em-heb is well known not to apply to any King of the latter part of the Twenty-sixth Dynasty, or of the Twenty-seventh; nor can it apply to any of the well-known viceroys, governors, and chiefs, of the time of the Persian domination mentioned by the Greek writers; neither to the Egyptians Inarus, Amyrtæus, Pausiris, and Thannyras; nor to the Persian governors Aryandes and Achæmenes, &c.; nor to that son of Amasis whose name is Ra-num-hat, the same as his father's prenomen. Hence we may suppose that the royal name Hor-em-heb is the name of a prince, or a viceroy, who exercised his power for a short time; and we may infer that he ruled in the early part of the Persian domination. From the size and splendour of the tomb, from its elaborate decoration, and from our finding no royal name but one of an unknown prince, and that but once occurring, we may reasonably suppose it to have been sculptured at a time when Egypt was under the dominion of foreigners; though it had not been long enough in that state to preclude the possibility of an Egyptian priest's making a magnificent tomb, but yet long enough for that tomb to have been sculptured; for if the tomb had been begun to be sculptured in the time of a native King, we should find royal rings containing his name, or left blank. The G. P. M. of which the commencement is recorded in the tomb of Pet-amen-apt is probably that which began B.C. 495. I offer these ideas respecting the date of the tomb with great diffidence. and as merely hypothetical; for it is by no means impossible that it may be removed to a later or earlier period by future discoveries.

I have already quoted the passage of Tacitus respecting the Phœnix, in which that writer says, after mentioning the appearances of the Phœnix in the times of Sesôstris and Amasis, that it appeared also in the reign of one of the Ptolemies, whom he calls "Ptolemy, who was the third Macedonian sovereign" (qui ex Macedonibus tertius regnavit). I might offer probable conjectures in explanation of this assertion, but I think it needless to do so. It may be supposed to refer to some one of the Panegyrical periods.

I cannot conclude this section without adding, that all the dates of the kinds above mentioned which I have seen on the monuments, or in printed copies of inscriptions, are perfectly in accordance with the system which I have put forth; and that I have suppressed no argument which I consider as opposing that system; but, on the contrary, have stated and explained all the objections that have occurred to me.

SECTION VII.

THE ROYAL PANEGYRIES.

IN the Greek inscription of the Rosetta Stone, Ptolemy Epiphanes is called "Lord of the Thirty-year Periods, like great Hephæstus:" ΚΥΡΙΟΥ ΤΡΙΑΚΟΝΤΑΕΤΗ-ΡΙΔΩΝ ΚΑΘΑΠΕΡ Ο ΗΦΑΙΣΤΟΣ Ο ΜΕΓΑΣ. The corresponding part of the hieroglyphic inscription is unfortunately lost; but we find the title in other inscriptions written in hieroglyphics, " Lord of the Royal Panegyries, like Ptah, or Phthah (*i. e.*, Hephæstus), Tatann." In the preceding passage, we find certain characters which signify " the Periods of Thirty Years," though the hieroglyphic symbol is merely a representation of the great hall in which the Panegyries of these periods were held. It is remarkable that the name is sometimes in the singular, and sometimes in the plural, and that the group in the plural appears sometimes to signify a single Thirty-year Period of Royal Panegyries. When I first ascertained the length of the G. P. M., I supposed it to be the same as the Thirty-year Period of Royal Panegyries; but differently named for some particular reason. But I found afterwards that this latter Period was connected with the reigns of Kings, by observing hieroglyphic inscriptions stating that some god had granted to a King to perform " a Period of Royal Panegyries;" thus evidently alluding to the Thirty-year Period of those Panegyries. I next observed, that those Kings who had long reigns, especially Papa

(Phiôps) and Rameses II., make frequent and remarkable mention of these Panegyries, whilst those who reigned but a few years do not notice them, or notice them but briefly. I then ascertained that the only records of particular years of Kings in which the commencements of Thirty-year Periods were celebrated render it probable that the Thirty-year Period of Royal Panegyries commenced in the first year of a King's reign, or in that year of his reign in which he first presided at the Royal Panegyries. A Thirty-year Period of Royal Panegyries is recorded to have commenced in the thirtieth year of the reign of Rameses II., and another in the thirty-third year of Thothmes III. The first seems obviously to point to the completion of thirty years from the Royal Panegyries of the year of the King's accession; and, upon consideration, it will be seen that the second is probably a record of the same purport. We know that Thothmes III. was for a time under the regency of Queen Amennumt, who doubtless presided at the Panegyries; and we know that this regency did not conclude before the King's third year, or a little later; whence we see that a period of thirty years would very probably commence in his thirty-third year.

From what I have just stated, compared with other circumstances connected with the Royal Panegyries, which I have also stated, especially that the celebration of a Period of Royal Panegyries was promised to the Egyptian Kings in the inscriptions of the temples, I can arrive at no other conclusion than that the Great Royal Panegyries were first celebrated at or about the completion of the King's thirtieth year, as counted from the Royal Panegyries of the year of his accession. The record of the time of Thothmes III. reads, " In

Sect. VII.] ROYAL PANEGYRIES OF RAMESES II. 73

the thirty-third year, on the second day of Mesori, the commencement of Periods of many and great Panegyries." This is the beginning of an inscription at El-Bersheh, in Middle Egypt, communicated to me by my friend Mr. Harris, of Alexandria, who has made important contributions to our knowledge of Egyptian archæology. A comparison of this with other inscriptions relating to the same subject plainly shows, that it can only relate to the commencement of a Thirty-year Period of Royal Panegyries. The usual manner of recording this event is by recording the commencement of the first of its subdivisions.

There are some very remarkable inscriptions of the reign of Rameses II., sculptured at Gebel-es-Silsileh, in Upper Egypt, which enable us to determine the length of certain subdivisions of the period which I have been just noticing. I give, in Plate III., No. 14, a copy of so much of one of these inscriptions as relates to the dates of Panegyries, from Champollion's "Monumens de l'Égypte et de la Nubie," Plate 116.

This inscription reads thus—

" Year 30. First (of) the Royal Panegyries."
" Year 34. Second (of) the Royal Panegyries."
" Year 37. Third of the Royal Panegyries."
" Year 40. Fourth of the Royal Panegyries."

Immediately after this, we read, " Of the Lord of Upper and Lower Egypt, Ra, the guardian (?) of justice, approved of the sun, lord of the rulers, Mee-amen Rameses [II.]." With respect to the translation which I have here given of this inscription, I must remark, that it is the ordinary group for the Panegyries I am now noticing which I render " Royal Panegyries;" that the years are the regnal years of

Rameses II.; and that the interpretation of a certain group as meaning "second" was first mentioned to me by Mr. Birch, of the British Museum, who believes that Dr. Hincks first mentioned it to him.

A very brief consideration of the inscription which I have just cited will show that the subdivisions of the Thirty-year Period of Royal Panegyries, which were marked by the celebration of what I may call " Little Royal Panegyries," could only have been periods of three Julian years, if they were of equal length. If such were the case, and if we suppose the first recorded in the inscription of Rameses II. to have commenced on the last day of the Vague Year, the succeeding ones would have fallen in the years there mentioned; and if this were the length of the subdivisions, each of them would correspond in length to two Divisions of the G. P. M., as the Thirty-year Period corresponded in length to the G. P. M.; thus confirming the durations that I have assigned to the latter Period and its Division. There is, however, one difficulty in this explanation of the Thirty-year Period of Royal Panegyries, and its subdivision. In what manner was the first thirty years of a King's reign divided? Although it is perfectly evident that the first Panegyry of much importance was the jubilee, which was celebrated in the King's thirtieth year, yet we must suppose that Little Royal Panegyries were previously celebrated. But the interval of nearly thirty Vague Years manifestly could not be divided into periods of three Julian years with exact precision. This will be explained if we suppose that the Royal Panegyries were celebrated on the occasion of the occurrence of some variable physical phenomenon, occurring at intervals of which the mean length would be a complete number of Julian years, though in particular instances they would somewhat differ in length one from another. From the place where the Royal Panegyries are most remarkably recorded, Gebel-es-Silsileh, the ancient Silsilis, where Nilus was particularly worshipped, and from the circumstance that both in the time of Thothmes III. and in that of Rameses II. (if one were celebrated late in his thirtieth year), these Panegyries were celebrated about midsummer, I think it most probable that they were partly celebrations of the first indication of the rise of the Nile (including the festival called by the Greeks the Niloa), since festivals celebrating such a phenomenon would have varied a little in time, if not fixed to a particular day, from the vagueness and slight irregularity of the event on which they would depend.

From the Thirty-year Period of Royal Panegyries, or from the Great Panegyrical Month, most probably originated the Thirty-year festivals of the Roman Emperors, which were called Tricennalia*.

* I have pointed out what I believe to be an indication of a Sixty-year Period in the shorter of the two Benee-Hasan inscriptions which I have already partly cited; and even if any do not agree with me as to the explanation of a certain group as signifying "The sixth of the twelve Asha," or "Egg-periods," it cannot be denied that there is great probability that the ancient Egyptians had a Sixty-year Period. If the First Great Panegyrical Month commenced with the First "Egg-period," the Eleventh and Twelfth G. P. M.'s coincided almost wholly with the Sixth "Egg-period." That the Egyptians made use of a Sixty-year Period, and connected that period with the crocodile and its eggs, is apparent from the statements of ancient writers. Plutarch says, that the crocodile's eggs are sixty in number, that they are sixty days before they are hatched, and that the longest life of the crocodile is sixty years. Iamblichus also states the number of the crocodile to be sixty,

which number he connects with the sun. Elian makes similar statements respecting the eggs of the crocodile, the time before hatching, the life of sixty years, and other particulars of the same kind. (See Wilkinson's "Ancient Egyptians," 2nd Series, Vol. ii., pp. 36, 233, 237.)

Horapollo Nilous (p. 12, ed. Cory) and others make mention of a Tetraëterid, or period of four Julian years, connected with the intercalary quarter of a day. As, however, we have no evidence of this period having been in use in the times of the Pharaohs, it is unnecessary to examine it. The ancient Egyptians may have had it so long as they made use of a year of 365 days and a quarter.

HORÆ ÆGYPTIACÆ.

PART II.
HISTORY.

SECTION I.

INTRODUCTORY OBSERVATIONS.

In the following pages I shall endeavour to present to the reader an outline of the History of Egypt during the time of the Pharaohs of the First Nineteen Dynasties, a period comprising about 1500 years, and ending about the date commonly assigned to the taking of Troy.

Before entering upon this portion of Egyptian history, I must consider the order of these Dynasties, a subject respecting which the learned of modern times have widely differed.

Every one allows that the Nineteenth Dynasty succeeded the Eighteenth, and that neither of these Dynasties was contemporary with any other: it is the order of the first seventeen Dynasties of Manetho's list that has been the cause of so many disputes, and it is this that I have to consider.

Manetho speaks of the rising of the Kings of the Thebaïd and of the other parts of Egypt against the Shepherds, themselves a Dynasty or Dynasties of Kings; and thus he plainly indicates his belief that there were at that time at least three contemporary Dynasties.

Other writers of ancient and modern times have affirmed some of the facts which I am about to prove, and have adduced arguments in favour of their assertions; but the proof from the monuments has hitherto been wanting. This proof I have now to give; and I beg that the reader will pay especial attention to it. I shall prove that the monuments establish the contemporaneousness of certain of the first seventeen Dynasties with others of the same portion of Manetho's list, by several records which have not hitherto been adduced as proofs of this important fact, and which develop the general scheme of the arrangement of these Dynasties in a most striking manner, while they signally confirm the Chronology ascertained in Part I.

It may be well here to remove a prejudice which some have thought to rest upon a foundation not easily shaken. It has been supposed that those Pharaohs who are styled in inscriptions of their own times Kings of all Egypt, or, more particularly, Kings of Upper and Lower Egypt, titles not uncommonly used, were sole Kings; and, consequently, that some of the first seventeen Dynasties ruled alone over all Egypt, without contemporaries. That this is an erroneous conclusion will be most satisfactorily proved by inscriptions which I shall have to cite, in which two contemporary Kings are mentioned, and one of them receives these titles. Even if we had not these proofs, it seems to me that this objection would not carry any weight, when we remember the parallel instances in the history of other nations, such as the title of King of Great Britain, France, and Ireland; and others too numerous to mention. Several Oriental Sovereigns of the present day arrogate to themselves titles far more extravagant, with respect to the extent of their rule, than those which certain of the Pharaohs assumed in calling themselves Kings of all Egypt.

The following table of the order of the first seventeen Dynasties was constructed by my uncle, Mr. E. W. Lane, in the year 1830. He founded it upon the evidence given by Manetho and others, that some of the early Dynasties were contemporary, and upon a consideration of the ordinal and other appellations (or numbers and names) by which those Dynasties are distinguished; for the interpretation of hieroglyphics was not then certain enough for him to obtain clear monumental evidence. When I commenced the study of hieroglyphics, he showed me this table; and, although he had discontinued that study for some years, he expressed his belief that his arrangement would be confirmed by the discoveries of others. After perusing some of the works of late authors, I became persuaded that his system was untenable; and that, if any of the Dynasties were contemporary, they were not contemporary in that order. Thus I relinquished it, and sought in the works of others a true scheme of Egyptian chronology; but sought in vain: I could find no system that would bear the test of comparison with the monuments. At last, after lamenting the time that had been lost in this fruitless search, I determined to study the monuments only, and to judge for myself; and, to my astonishment, I found everything confirm my uncle's theory, until, by degrees, proving point after point, I at last became convinced that the system was altogether correct. *Thus I came to the conclusions which I have adopted after having long entertained the strongest prejudices against them.* I now subjoin the table.

Thinites.	Memphites.	Elephantinites.	Heracleopolites.	Diospolites.	Xoites.	Shepherds.
Dyn. Yrs.	Dyn. Yrs.	Dys. Dyn. Yrs.	Dyn. Yrs.	Dyn. Yrs.	Dyn. Years.	Dyn. Yrs.
1st 253	3rd 214					
2nd 302	4th 284	5th 248	9th 409	11th 59	... ...	
	6th 203	... ...	10th 185	12th 160	... ...	15th ⎫
	7th ... 70	... ...	... ...	13th 184	14th 184 or 284	16th ⎬ 511
	8th 146	... ...	... ...	17th 151	... ...	17th ⎭
555	847 70	248	594	554	184 or 284	511

My uncle has assigned 511 years to the Shepherd-Dynasties, instead of the sum of the durations of those Dynasties in the lists, because Manetho states that the whole period of the Shepherd-rule was 511 years. The length of those Dynasties I shall presently consider. He has in this table given the numbers of years according to Africanus's transcript of Manetho's list, excepting in the case just noticed. It will be afterwards seen that these numbers need corrections: my uncle gave them in his table because he considered them in general the most correct. What he intended to be shown by that table will appear more clearly in the following arrangement of the Dynasties, also made by him: the only alteration that I have made in this is in the case of the Seventeenth Dynasty, which I hold to have been a single Dynasty, of Shepherds; not a double Dynasty, of Diospolites and Shepherds: but this does not affect the general system.

$$\left.\begin{matrix}\text{1st}\\\text{2nd}\end{matrix}\right\}\left\{\begin{matrix}\text{3rd}\\\text{4th}\end{matrix}\right.\ \text{5th}$$

$$\left.\begin{matrix}\text{6th}\\\text{7th}\\\text{8th}\end{matrix}\right\}---\left\{\begin{matrix}\text{9th}\\\ \\\text{10th}\end{matrix}\right\}\left\{\begin{matrix}\text{11th}\\\text{12th}\\\text{13th}\end{matrix}\right\}\text{14th}\left\{\begin{matrix}\text{15th}\\\text{16th}\\\text{17th}\end{matrix}\right.$$

This table exhibits the First and Second Dynasties as for the most part contemporary with the Third and Fourth; the Fourth with the Fifth; the Sixth, Seventh, and Eighth with the Ninth and Tenth; the Ninth and Tenth with the Eleventh, Twelfth, and Thirteenth; the Twelfth and Thirteenth with the Fourteenth; and the Fourteenth with the Fifteenth, Sixteenth, and Seventeenth.

This arrangement of the first seventeen Dynasties rests, particularly, on the following grounds:—The

Memphites of the Fourth Dynasty are clearly shown by the monuments to have been in part contemporary with the Elephantinites of the Fifth. The Diospolites of the Eleventh and Twelfth Dynasties are likewise shown to have been in part contemporary with the Heracleopolites of the Ninth, and the Shepherds of the Fifteenth; and the latter part of the Fifteenth Dynasty is also shown to have been contemporary with the latter part of the Fifth. The Fifteenth Dynasty I also find to have immediately, or almost immediately, succeeded the Sixth Dynasty. The arrangement of five columns of the table I consider as thus established from monumental evidence. The Thinite kingdom cannot be supposed to have commenced long before the Memphite. This will plainly appear from what I have to state respecting the Era of Mênês, in Section III. of this Part; from a consideration of my explanation of the Tablet of Abydos, in the same section; and from an inspection of the hieroglyphic Table of the first seventeen Dynasties, at the end of this work, in which it will be seen that, by assigning average lengths to the reigns of the Thinite Kings, we find that the end of the Second Dynasty comes almost exactly to the point where the Twelfth Dynasty begins both in that Table and in the Tablet of Abydos. Other reasons also will be found in the course of this work. The Xoite kingdom probably arose about the time of the Shepherd-invasion, shortly after which event the Fifteenth Dynasty commenced. Those propositions which I state to be proved by the monuments will be fully developed in the ensuing inquiries.

The true arrangement of the first seventeen Dynasties indicates the following leading historical facts.

The Thinites were the first Egyptian Kings, and the

first of them, Mênês, was undoubtedly sole King of Egypt. Soon after the establishment of the Thinite kingdom, Lower Egypt, it appears, became an independent state, and Memphis was its capital. About two centuries after this event both the Thinite and Memphite kingdoms appear to have been dismembered by the establishment of the Elephantinite Dynasty; and many years afterwards, by that of the Heracleopolite and Diospolite Dynasties. Not long after the time of the commencement of the Diospolite kingdom, another kingdom, the Xoite, appears to have been founded, in Lower Egypt; and about the same time, a warlike eastern tribe of Pastors, to whose successive chiefs the Egyptians gave the appellation of Shepherd-Kings, invaded Egypt, and, favoured by its divided state, made all the native princes tributary to them, choosing Memphis as their capital. These, and other tribes of Pastors, whose Kings compose the Fifteenth, Sixteenth, and Seventeenth Dynasties, ruled in Egypt for more than five hundred years.

SECTION II.

THE LISTS OF MANETHO AND THE MONUMENTS.

IN the present section I have to notice the lists of the first seventeen Dynasties given by Manetho, and those found on the monuments.

I first give Manetho's list of the first seventeen Dynasties, arranged, approximatively, in the order of contemporaneousness. Other lists will be given in subsequent places, and I shall frequently have occasion to comment upon all the lists here mentioned.

I. THE FIRST FIVE DYNASTIES.

THINITES.
First Dynasty.

Eight Kings, who reigned 253[a] years.

1. Mênês	. . . .	62[b]
2. Athôthis	. . . .	57[c]
3. Kenkenês	. . . .	31[d]
4. Uenephês	. . . .	23[e]
5. Usaphaidos[f]	. . . .	20
6. Miebis[g]	. . . .	26
7. Semempsês[h]	. . . .	18
8. Bi ênchês[i]	. . . .	26
	Sum . .	263[j]

VARIATIONS.

[a]252, E.—[b]60, E. G.—30, E. A.—[c]27, E. G.—25, E.—[d]39, E.—[e]42, E.—[f]Usaphaês, E. or Usaphais, E. G.— Miêbês, E. or Niêis, E.—[g]Miebês, E. A.—[i]Ubienthês, E. G.—Vibesthes, E.—[j]258, E. G.—226, E. A.

Note.—The sum of the years of the reigns added up differs from the sum at the head of the Dynasty in Eus. and Afr.

MEMPHITES.
Third Dynasty.

Nine Kings,[a] who reigned 214[b] years.

1. Necherôphês[c]	. . . .	28
2. Tosorthros[d]	. . . .	29
3. Tyreis	. . . .	7
4. Mesôchris	. . . .	17
5. Sôyphis	. . . .	16
6. Tosertasis	. . . .	19
7. Achês	. . . .	42
8. Sêphuris	. . . .	30
9. Kerpherês	. . . .	26
	Sum . . .	214

VARIATIONS.

[a]Eight Kings, E.—[b]198, E. G.—197, E. A.—[c]Necherôchis, E.—[d]Sesorthos, E.

Note.—Eus. only mentions the first two Kings of this Dyn. by name, and does not state the length of their reigns.

ELEPHANTINITES.

Sect. II.] MANETHO'S LISTS. 87

Second Dynasty.

Nine Kings, who reigned 302ᵃ years.

1. Boêthosᵇ 38
2. Chaiechôsᶜ 39
3. Binôthrisᵈ 47
4. Tlas 17
5. Sethenês 41
6. Chairês 17
7. Nepherchêrês 25
8. Sesôchris 48
9. Chêês 30
                          ———
                    Sum . . . 302

VARIATIONS.

ᵃ297, E.—ᵇBôchos, E.—ᶜChôis, E. G.—Cechous, E. A.—ᵈBiophis, E.

Note.—Eus. mentions only the first, second, third, and eighth Kings of this Dynasty by their names, and only states the length of the reign of the eighth, which is the same as in Afr.

Fourth Dynasty.

Eight Kingsᵃ, who reigned 274ᵇ years.

1. Sôris 29
2. Sûphis 63
3. Sûphis 66
4. Mencherês 63
5. Rhatoisês 25
6. Bicheris 22
7. Sebercherês 7
8. Thamphthis 9
                          ———
                    Sum . . . 284

VARIATIONS.

ᵃ17 Kings, E.—ᵇ448, E.

Note.—The sum of the years of the reigns, added up, differs from the sum at the end of the Dyn. in Afr. Eus. owns no King of this Dyn. but Sûphis, whom he calls the third King, and to whom he ascribes this which Afr. ascribes to Sûphis I.

Fifth Dynasty.

Eight Kingsᵃ; who reigned 248 years.

1. Usercherês 28
2. Sephrês 13
3. Nephercherês 20
4. Sisirês 7
5. Chêrês 20
6. Rhathurês 44
7. Menchêrês 9
8. Tancherês 44
9. Onnosᵇ 33
                          ———
                    Sum . . . 218

VARIATIONS.

ᵃ31 Kings, E.—ᵇObnos, Afr.

Note.—The number of Kings at the head of the Dyn. is one less than those whose names are given.—Eus. does not state the duration of this Dyn., and mentions only two Kings, Iôês (G.), or Othus (A.), and Phiôps, whom he calls the first and fourth Kings. These Kings are obviously, and really belonging to the Sixth Dyn.

II. THE SIXTH AND ELEVEN SUBSEQUENT DYNASTIES.

MEMPHITES.	HERACLEOPOLITES.	DIOSPOLITES.	XOITES.		SHEPHERDS.
Sixth Dynasty.	*Ninth Dynasty.*	*Eleventh Dynasty.*			
Six Kings, who reigned 203 years.	Nineteen Kings[a], who reigned 109[b] years.	Sixteen Kings, who reigned 43 years. After whom Ammenemês 16.			
1. Othoês . . . 30	1. Achthoês[c].				
2. Phios . . . 53					
3. Methusuphis 7	VARIATIONS.				
4. Phiôps . . . 100	a 4 Kings, E.—b 100,				
5. Menthesûphis 1	E.—Achthoês, E. G.				
6. Nitôkris . . 12	—Ochthois, E. A.				
Sum . . . 203					
Notes.—In the text of Africanus's list, as it now stands, we find Nitôkris for Nitôkris, an obvious mistake.—Eusebius mentions only Queen Nitôkris in this Dyn.			*Fourteenth Dynasty.*	*Fifteenth Dynasty.*	*Sixteenth Dynasty.*
			Seventy-six Kings, who reigned 184[a] eyars.	Six Kings, who reigned 284 eyars.	Thirty-two Kings[a], who reigned 518 years.
		Twelfth Dynasty.	VARIATIONS.	1. Saitês . . . 19	VARIATIONS.
		Seven Kings, who reigned 160[a] eyars.	a 184 or 484, E. G.— 484, E. A.	2. Bnôn . . . 44	a 5 Theban Kings, who reigned 190 years, Eus.
		1. Sesonchôsis[b] . 46		3. Pachnan . . 61	
		2. Ammanemês . 38		4. Staan . . . 50	
		3. Sesôstris . . 48		5. Iânias . . . 49	
		4. Lacharês[c] . . 8		6. Apôbis . . . 61	
		5. Amerês . . 8		Sum . . . 284	
		6. Amerês . . 8			
		7. Skemiophris . 4			
		Sum . . . 160			

[Sect. II.] MANETHO'S LISTS. 89

Seventh Dynasty.
Seventy Kings[a], who reigned 70[b] days.

VARIATIONS.
[a] 5 Kings, E.—[b] 75 days, E. G.—75 years, E. A.

Eighth Dynasty.
Twenty-seven Kings[a], who reigned 146[b] years.

VARIATIONS.
[a] 5 Kings, E. G.—9 Kings, E. A.—[b] 100, E.

VARIATIONS.
[a] 245, E.—[b] Gesongosis, Afr.—[c] Lamaris, E. G.—Lampares, E. A.
Note.—Eus. gives no Kings' names after Lamaris; but adds that his successors reigned 42 years. Thus the sum would be 182, not 245, years.

Thirteenth Dynasty.
Sixty Kings, who reigned 453 years.

Tenth Dynasty.
Nineteen Kings, who reigned 185 years.

VARIATIONS.
The lists of this Dyn. given by Joseph'us & Eus. are so different from that of Afr. that I shall here insert them in full. Eus. calls this the 16th Dyn.
The list of Jos. is:—

	YRS. M.
1. Saïtes	19
2. Béôn	44
3. Apachnas	36
4. Aphis	61
5. Iannas	50 1
6. Assis	49 2
Sum	259 10

Eusebius's 17th Dyn. is of Shepherd-Kings, who reigned 103 years.

1. Saïtes	19
2. Bnôn	40
3. Aphôphis	14
4. Archlés	30
Sum	103

E. G. In the Arm. version, Archlés is put before Aphôphis.

Seventeenth Dynasty.
Forty-three Diospolite Kings and forty-three Shepherd-Kings[a], who reigned 151 years.

VARIATIONS.
[a] Diospolite Kings, who reigned 250 years, Eus.
Note.—Eus. calls this the Fifteenth Dyn.

In the preceding tables, I have given the lists of Manetho according to the transcript of Africanus, as being the most correct extant; and I have added the most important variations from the Greek text and Armenian translation of Eusebius's Chronicle, with a list of the Fifteenth Dynasty from the fragments of Manetho preserved by Josephus, and a few variations of the text of Africanus. In the abbreviations which I have employed, E. stands for the Greek text and Armenian translation of Eusebius when they agree; E. G. for the Greek text, and E. A. for the Armenian translation.

At the end of this volume will be found a table of the hieroglyphic names of all the Kings that I have found to belong to particular Dynasties, from the First to the Seventeenth inclusive; the Dynasties and Kings being there arranged in their proper relative places, according to the monuments, which seldom enable us to determine the exact points of contemporaneousness in two or more Dynasties; and the spaces allotted to particular Kings being proportioned to the lengths of their reigns in some particular and remarkable cases; average length, deduced from the length of the Dynasty, and the number of its Kings, being indicated in other cases. Sir Gardner Wilkinson has most kindly offered me the use of the wood-blocks from which the names in the table above mentioned, as well as most of the names of Kings which occur in this work, are printed.

The errours in Manetho's lists, and the manner in which the monuments assist us in verifying or correcting those lists, will be discussed in many places throughout this portion of the present work. The instances of corruption by copyists, to be noticed hereafter, plainly show us that we cannot rely upon the accuracy of the numbers in Manetho's Dynasties as they now stand, and that we must therefore correct that historian's lists as far as possible from the dates and other records on the monuments. I must also distinctly state, that I place no reliance upon Manetho in any case in which he is not in some degree confirmed by the monuments or other trustworthy ancient authority. The corruption of his text, by copyists or epitomizers, has probably been partly intentional and partly unintentional; but I suppose it to have been in a great measure effected before the times of Josephus, Theophilus of Antioch, Africanus, and Eusebius; whose quotations and abstracts of Manetho have still further suffered by the carelessness of later copyists.

There are several other lists of Egyptian Kings, preserved on the monuments and in papyri: on the former, in hieroglyphic characters; in the latter, in hieratic.

The chief of these lists are the List of the Chamber of Kings, and that called the Tablet of Abydos. The former, which contained sixty-one royal names, belonging to the Sixth, Ninth, Eleventh, Twelfth, Thirteenth, and Fifteenth, Dynasties, and which other writers have been utterly unable to explain, most remarkably confirms the arrangement of the Dynasties which I have adopted. It is a monument of the reign of Thothmes III., the fifth King of the Eighteenth Dynasty, by whose order it was sculptured, in a chamber of the great temple of the metropolis of that time. The latter list (that of Abydos) contained fifty-two names (two of which are of one King) of Thinite and Diospolite Kings, as will soon be shown. In both lists, many names are erased. There are also many other shorter lists on the monuments, containing from two to fourteen Kings' names, and dating from the time of the Fourth Dynasty to that of the Twentieth.

The Royal Turin Papyrus is a hieratic manuscript which, from what remains of it, seems to have contained the first seventeen Dynasties, with the lengths of the Kings' reigns, generally in years, months, and days, but sometimes, in years only; with the commencements of Dynasties indicated. Most unhappily it is in a very mutilated state, so that little information has hitherto been derived from it. I shall, however, have to notice some important facts which are to be learnt from this record, and to show that it affords a most remarkable confirmation of the scheme of contemporary Dynasties which I have founded upon the monuments.

SECTION III.

HISTORY OF THE PERIOD BEFORE THE SHEPHERD INVASION.

MENES was the first King of Egypt, according to Manetho, Herodotus, and Diodorus Siculus. His hieroglyphic name, which reads Menee, heads the list

at the Rameseum of El-Kurneh. It is also given in the Royal Turin Papyrus as the name of the first mortal King.

There is a very remarkable passage in the Euterpe of Herodotus*, which has been supposed to be of great importance towards the elucidation of the Egyptian Chronology. After having spoken of the number of generations from the first King to Sethôn the priest of Hephæstus, and said that in the interval

---

* The list which Herodotus has given of the most remarkable of the Pharaohs, as received from the Egyptian priests, though it presents several inaccuracies, plainly shews us a fact too remarkable to be passed over without notice: that the priests read to him a list of the most celebrated of the Kings of Upper Egypt, and then a list of those of Lower Egypt: and his chief errour lay in his supposing that the latter succeeded the former.

from the former to the latter no god had appeared in a human form, the historian adds, that " they [the priests] said, that in this time the sun had risen four times out of its usual places: where it now sets, it had twice risen; and where it now rises it had twice set;" and he goes on to say, that these events had produced no physical changes in Egypt. (Ἐν τοίνυν τούτῳ τῷ χρόνῳ τετράκις ἔλεγον ἐξ ἠθέων τὸν ἥλιον ἀνατεῖλαι· ἔνθα τε νῦν καταδύεται, ἐνθεῦτεν δὶς ἐπαντεῖλαι· καὶ ἔνθεν νῦν ἀνατέλλει, ἐνθαῦτα δὶς καταδῦναι· καὶ οὐδὲν τῶν κατ᾽ Αἴγυπτον ὑπὸ ταῦτα ἑτεροιωθῆναι, οὔτε τὰ ἐκ τῆς γῆς, οὔτε τὰ ἐκ τοῦ ποταμοῦ σφι γινόμενα, οὔτε τὰ ἀμφὶ νούσους, οὔτε τὰ κατὰ τοὺς θανάτους.) Many attempts have been made to explain this passage; but none of them is satisfactory; and I am convinced that the reader will agree with me that the explanation which I am about to offer (supported by most remarkable evidence) is the true one.

It is evident that the priests told Herodotus that great periods had elapsed since the time of Mênês, the first King; and that, in the interval from his reign to that of Sethôn, the *solar risings* of stars, that is to say, their manifestations, had twice fallen on those days of the Vague Year on which their settings fell in their own time; and *vice versâ;* and that the historian, by a natural mistake, supposed they spoke of the sun itself. This would place Mênês at or before cir. B.C. 2760 to 2640 and later than cir. B.C. 3490 to 3370. Sethôn was reigning in Egypt about B.C. 713; and therefore the interval from his time to that of Herodotus is not sufficiently long to affect the calculation based upon the historian's statement. Herodotus was in Egypt about the year B.C. 450.

Porphyry says, that the Egyptian year, by which he

GENESIS OF THE WORLD.

means the Sothic Year, commenced with the rising of Sothis, which marked the genesis of the world. (Αἰγυπτίοις δὲ ἀρχὴ ἔτους οὐχ ὑδροχόος, ὡς 'Ρωμαίοις, ἀλλὰ καρκίνος. Πρὸς γὰρ τῷ καρκίνῳ ἡ Σῶθις, ἣν κυνὸς ἀστέρα ῞Ελληνές φασι. Νουμηνία δὲ αὐτοῖς ἡ Σώθεως ἀνατολή, γενέσεως κατάρχουσα τῆς εἰς τὸν κόσμον*.) It is scarcely necessary to remark that he speaks of Aquarius instead of Capricornus as the sign of the Winter Solstice by an evident oversight. Perhaps he obtained the information just mentioned, respecting Sothis and the genesis of the world, from Manetho's works, one of which, concerning " Archæology and Piety," (περὶ ἀρχαϊσμοῦ καὶ εὐσεβείας,) he quotes in his treatise de Abstinentiâ.

Solinus tells us, as on the authority of the priests, that the time of the rising of Sothis was the birth of the world ; but he is mistaken in fixing upon what was in his time the conventional day of the rising of Sothis. (Verum omnem abscessus originem de sole concipi, primosque fieri excessus tumoris, cum per cancrum sol vehatur : postmodum triginta ejus partibus evolutis, ubi ingressus leonem ortus sirios excitavit, propulso omni fluore tantam vim amnis erumpere. Quod tempus sacerdotes natalem mundi indicarunt, id est, inter tertium decimum Calendas Augustas & undecimum†.) There is another passage concerning the rising of Sothis, &c., which is generally supposed also to refer to the genesis of the world. It is in the manuscript work of Vettius Valens, an astrologer. I do not cite it, as the meaning is contested, and somewhat obscure.

I have given my reasons in the first part of this work for asserting that the first Great Panegyrical

* De Antro Nympharum, 24. † Cap. 32.

Year commenced, and the Calendar of the Panegyries was instituted, in the year B.C. 2717; and that the manifestation of Sothis then fell in the first month of the Vague Year, and was consequently celebrated on the first day of that month. Hence it is evident that this era was not instituted for purely astronomical and chronological purposes, but also to mark a historical period. If it had not been so, it would have commenced with the day of the manifestation of Sothis, like the first Sothic Cycle; or, possibly, with the day of the Summer Solstice; neither of which was the case. This is evidently the era to which the statement of the priests to Herodotus points; for it falls within the interval obtained from his statement and within the smaller interval indicated in the works of Porphyry and Solinus, and is the earliest date that is deduced from the monuments.

To recapitulate these arguments: the Egyptian priests made a statement to Herodotus, from which I find that Mênês began to reign in some one of the eight hundred and fifty years from cir. B.C. 3490 to 2640: and Porphyry and Solinus say, that Sothis was the star of the genesis of the world, indicating that the manifestation of Sothis then fell, or was celebrated, on the first day of the Vague Year; thus shortening the eight hundred and fifty years to about one hundred and twenty. I have before spoken of the Era of Mênês as the same as the genesis of the world. This needs explanation. Herodotus himself, the Royal Turin Papyrus, and Manetho, most distinctly tell us that Mênês was the first mortal King. His accession is the date of the origin of the Egyptian race; and therefore, since they thought themselves the most ancient of men, is what they called the genesis of the world. The date of the commencement of the first Great Panegyrical Year, and of the institution of the Calendar of the Panegyries, is B.C. 2717, a year which undoubtedly falls not only within the period indicated by Herodotus, but also within the smaller limits obtained from the statements of Porphyry and Solinus.

Thus we see that the Era of Mênês, which was probably the date of that King's accession, or at least fell in his reign, was the date of the commencement of the first Great Panegyrical Year, B.C. 2717. I cannot omit here to notice how this date is corroborated by the records of other nations.

The Septuagint Chronology dates the Dispersion of mankind about the year B.C. 2758; that is, about forty-one years before the Era of Mênês.

The Bible-narrative indicates, that an Assyro-Babylonian kingdom was founded by Nimrod shortly after the Dispersion. The traditions and histories of the Assyrians and Babylonians respecting this part of their national existence are almost entirely lost: the history of Berossus is only known to us by a few fragments: but from these we learn that the period of tradition ended, and that of history began, some time after the Septuagint-date of the Dispersion. The reckoning by the mythic divisions of time of the Chaldæans, the sari, neri, and sossi, ends, and that by years begins, with the termination of the first Chaldæan kingdom and the conquest of Babylon by the Medes, an event which appears from the numbers and reigns to have taken place about the year B.C. 2500, or somewhat later. The origin of the Assyrian Empire, according to Ctesias and his followers, (excepting Eusebius,) dates about the year B.C. 2200; but their statements are of doubtful authority, to say the least. The Persians and Medes have preserved no ancient traditions respecting the period before Arbaces. The earliest Median Kings mentioned in history are those who reigned at Babylon after its capture, (cir. B.C. 2500,) though Berossus speaks of Median Kings during the traditional period. The first Persian King of whom we have any record is Chedorlaomer, who made two expeditions with other Kings into Palestine and the neighbouring countries, between the years B.C. 2095 and 2071, according to Hales's Chronology, slightly corrected by me. What the modern Persians say of their ancient history is purely poetical, and contains as little truth as the Greek accounts of the exploits of Hercules and Perseus.

Leaving the nations in the immediate vicinity of the land of Shinar, the original seat of the human race, we find the traditions and histories of other nations, not far distant, pointing to a period little subsequent to the date of the Dispersion, or indicating their origin at that time.

The priests of the Tyrian Hercules told Herodotus that Tyre was built, and the temple of their god founded, at the same time; and that since Tyre was first inhabited, two thousand three hundred years had intervened. This would place the foundation of Tyre about the year B.C. 2750, shortly after the Dispersion.

The Arabs have no ancient history, and scarcely any veritable ancient tradition, excepting that they have preserved the memory of their descent from Joktan, and from Ishmael.

It is well known that the history and traditions of

other nations point to more recent periods than those I have just mentioned, and therefore it is unnecessary to consider them.

Before noticing the actions ascribed to Mênês, I must not omit to mention the mythical relation of the Egyptians concerning the time before Mênês. As we learn from Eusebius, Manetho states in his history, that the gods, demi-gods or heroes, and manes, reigned during a vast period of twenty-four thousand and nine hundred years before Mênês. Similar statements are found in the works of Herodotus and Diodorus; and some have attempted to explain these mythic periods by supposing that the year was anciently called a month, and that these are periods of months, not of years; but, although this opinion has been held by several ancient writers, it is evidently at variance with the Egyptian system. From all this it is perfectly clear that the Egyptians had neither history nor tradition of their own existence as a nation before Mênês.

Respecting Mênês, Manetho, according to Eusebius, tells us that he made a foreign expedition, and acquired renown; and, moreover, that he was killed by a hippopotamus, as Africanus also tells us in his version of Manetho's lists. The sculptures and paintings of the tombs of the ancient Egyptians show us that hunting the hippopotamus was one of the favourite sports of that people, and it was probably in indulging in it that Mênês lost his life. The expedition of Mênês, the earliest recorded in history, was probably made to repress the incursions of some wandering tribe on the eastern frontier of Lower Egypt. (On the first occasion of mentioning the short historical notices which occur in the lists of Manetho, it is necessary to remark, that we cannot always be certain that they are derived from that historian's work.) Diodorus Siculus relates*, that Mênês, whom he calls Mênas, first instructed the Egyptians in religion, and so changed their simple manners, that Tnephachthos, the father of Bokchoris the Wise, finding from experience the happiness of a frugal life and the evils of luxury, inscribed a curse against him in the temple of Jupiter (or Amen-ra) at Thebes.

Herodotus † ascribes to Mênês more useful actions than those mentioned by Diodorus: he says that he founded Memphis, after he had diverted the course of the river by raising a dike. Probably he did not change the course of the river, but built Memphis on an island, and closed the southern end of the western branch; but this is only conjecture, as we cannot say what was the exact course of the Nile at that remote period. The situation of Memphis, as the capital of Egypt, was wisely chosen; and it appears to have been long the chief city in extent and population. Herodotus also tells us that Mênês founded the temple of Vulcan, or Ptah. Some remains of a temple which was probably dedicated to Ptah may still be seen on the site of Memphis.

Mênês is said by Manetho to have been of This; and the Kings of his Dynasty, as well as those of the succeeding one, are called by that author Thinites. The ancient city of This was situated near to Abydos, in Upper Egypt. No remains of its monuments are known to have been preserved to the present day.

I have recognised the names of certain of the Thinite Kings in the Tablet of Abydos. The table here annexed will shew the arrangement, and what were till

* I. 45.   † II. 99.

lately preserved, of the names comprised in that important monument, the first division of which I am the first to explain. My explanation of this tablet, shewing that it contained a complete list of the Thinite Kings, is founded upon internal evidence which it presents, and confirmed by the fact of its being found in the neighbourhood of the site of the Thinite capital. Besides, it would be difficult to find any other place or places, before the Twelfth Dynasty, in which the Kings here preceding that Dynasty could be introduced. The Kings' names contained in the first two lines of this tablet are given in Plate IV., No. 1.

	1. ——	27. ——	
	2. ——	28. ——	
	3. ——	29. ——	
	4. ——	30. ——	
	5. ——	31. ——	
	6. ——	32. ——	
	7. ——	33. ——	
	8. ——	34. ——	
	9. ——	35. Nub-kau-ra.	
TABLET OF ABYDOS.	10. ——	36. Sha-ter-ra.	REPETITIONS OF THE NOMEN AND PRENOMEN OF MEE-AMEN RAMESES.
	11. ——	37. Sha-kau-ra.	
	12. ——	38. Ma-en-ra.	
	13. . . . . f	39. Ma-tu-ra.	
	14. . . neter-ka.	40. Neb . . . . ra.	
	15. Men-ka-ra.	41. Ser-ka-ra.	
	16. Nufre-ka-ra.	42. Naa-ter-ka-ra.	
	17. Nufre-ka-ra. Nebee.	43. Naa-ter-en-ra.	
	18. Tet-ka-ra. Ma.	44. Men-ter-ra.	
	19. Nufre-ka-ra. Khentub.	45. Naä-teru-ra.	
	20. Mer-en-hor.	46. Men-teru-ra	
	21. Snufre-ka.	47. Ma-neb-ra.	
	22. Ka-en-ra.	48. Ser-teru-ra setep-en-ra.	
	23. Nufre-ka-ra. Rerer.	49. Men . . . . ra.	
	24. . . . . nufre-ka.	50. Ma-men-ra.	
	25. Nufre-ka-en-seb. Papa.	51. Seser-ma-ra.	
	26. Snufre-ka. Annu.	52. Mee-amen Rameses.	

The sixteenth name in this list is Nufre-ka-ra; and Nephercherês is the fifteenth Thinite King, according to Africanus's version of Manetho's list: his predecessor, Men-ka-ra, is called Chairês in the same list. The sixth King after Nufre-ka-ra in the Tablet is Ka-en-ra, the Chenerês of Manetho, (in Africanus,) who makes him the second successor of Nephercherês. He is preceded in the Tablet by Snufre-ka, perhaps the same as Sesôchris, whom Manetho (in Africanus) makes the predecessor of Chenerês. After Ka-en-ra, we find in the Tablet the names of four other Kings, evidently belonging to the same Dynasty. I conclude that it continued to the commencement of the Twelfth Dynasty, since there are only seven effaced rings in which the names of the Kings of the Eleventh Dynasty could have been inscribed, had that Dynasty preceded the Twelfth in the Tablet; and eight of its Kings are found in the list of the Chamber of Kings. Hence it appears that the Second Dynasty continued until the commencement of the Shepherd-Kingdom and Twelfth Dynasty. It is to be remarked that the first uneffaced ring in the second line of the Tablet of Abydos is that containing the prenomen of Amenemha II. I reckon the last ring of the Second Dynasty to be the third preceding this, since we cannot suppose that Amenemha I. (the first colleague of Seserteseu I.) was omitted. Fourteen names of the Kings of the Second Dynasty were preserved partly or wholly in the Tablet of Abydos at the time that Sir Gardner Wilkinson made his invaluable copy *; three of these being partly erased; the rest perfect. The recognition of names of Kings of the Second Dynasty in the Tablet of Abydos, indicating that the first line of that

* Materia Hieroglyphica, Part II., Pl. IX.

tablet and part of the second consisted of an entire list of the Thinite Kings, thirty-two in number, will, I think, be regarded as an interesting and important discovery. It is further worthy of remark that most of the names of Thinite Kings after Nufre-ka-ra in the Tablet are of a compound form, a prenomen and nomen in one ring, and that this is accounted for by their belonging to a period partly preceding, and partly synchronous with, the Sixth, Ninth, and Eleventh Dynasties, in which we first find Kings with separate prenomens.

The son and successor of Mênês was Athôthis, who was the second King of the First Dynasty. Manetho, according to Africanus and Eusebius, tells us that this King built the palace at Memphis, and that he was a physician, and left the anatomical books. This is a very remarkable statement, as it affirms that the Thinites had possession of Memphis for some years, and also that the Egyptians had made some progress in the art of writing, and in medicine, at that early period. The name of Athôthis, the etymology of which must be A-thoth, the son of Thoth, or Hermes, shews the antiquity of some part of the ancient Egyptian religion: it seems, however, that all the details of the system were not completed until the reign of Kaiechôs, the second King of the Second Dynasty, from a statement in the lists which I shall soon have to consider. The name of Athôthis, in a much injured state, is supposed to be found in the Royal Turin Papyrus.

The Third Dynasty evidently commenced, and Memphis became independent, during, or soon after, the reign of Athôthis. As, however, the time of this occurrence cannot as yet be exactly determined, I shall continue the history of the Thinite Kingdom during the First and Second Dynasties, before entering upon the consideration of the history of the Memphite Kingdom.

Respecting Kenkenês, the third King of the First Dynasty, we know nothing more than that he was the son of Athôthis. (Afr. and Eus.) We are told that Uenephês, his successor, built the Pyramids near Kôchômê. I have been unable to find any name which I could reasonably suppose to be that of Kôchômê among the names of the Egyptian cities found on the monuments, or mentioned by Greek, Roman, or Copt, writers. This is the earliest notice of Pyramids. We are told nothing more respecting the Kings of this Dynasty, and the events of their reigns, excepting that a famine afflicted Egypt in the reign of the King last mentioned; and that there happened a very great plague ($\phi\theta o\rho\grave{a}$ $\mu\epsilon\gamma\acute{\iota}\sigma\tau\eta$) in that of Semempsês, the seventh King of the Dynasty, and, as Eusebius adds, many remarkable events.—Such are the fragments which have come down to us, in Manetho's lists, of the history of the First Dynasty, and it is to be feared that the hieroglyphic inscriptions will furnish us with few, if any, more, owing to the remoteness of the period, and the want of monuments which we can certainly ascribe to this Dynasty.

In considering the history of the next Dynasty, I shall not distinguish the statements which are given in Manetho's lists, as no other ancient historian has preserved any records of it, and therefore no mistake can arise. In the time of the first King of the Second Dynasty, Boêthos, we are told that a chasm of the earth opened at Bubastis, and many perished. This is a remarkable statement, as Egypt is seldom subject to earthquakes, but often to the shocks of earthquakes which happen in Syria. These are, however, sometimes so severe as to cause much destruction among the mosques and houses of the Egyptians in the present day. Similar shocks are recorded by the Arab historians of Egypt, and the manner in which some of the ancient temples have fallen shews that their accounts are not exaggerated. During my residence in Egypt, I felt several shocks, one of which was so violent that about seventy houses in Cairo were rendered uninhabitable; several of them being entirely ruined; and much injury was done to the mosques. Similar, though less severe, shocks are by no means unfrequent; but I am not aware that there is any record, besides that in Manetho's lists, of these shocks being ever accompanied in Egypt by an opening of the earth, though such occurrences are not rare in Syria.

We are told that in the reign of the next King, Kaiechôs, the bulls Apis, in Memphis, and Mnevis, in Heliopolis, and the Mendesian goat, were called gods. ($\dot{\epsilon}\nu o\mu i\sigma\theta\eta\sigma a\nu$ $\epsilon\dot{\iota}\nu a\iota$ $\theta\epsilon o\dot{\iota}$, Afr. $\theta\epsilon o\dot{\iota}$ $\dot{\epsilon}\nu o\mu i\sigma\theta\eta\sigma a\nu$, Eus.) From this it seems that the Egyptian religion was not completely developed until the time of Kaiechôs, or after his time; and that the great Ritual was not before composed.

In the reign of Binôthris, the next King, we are told that it was adjudged that women could reign. This law was certainly in force at a later period; for we find from Manetho and the monuments that there were at least two Queens during the first eighteen Dynasties.

Nothing is related of the history of the next three Kings, who are called "Tlas," "Sethenês," and "Chairês." According to my explanation of the Tablet of Abydos, the name belonging to the first of these three Kings is almost wholly erased, but the last character remains, and is the cerastes; and one of the few Kings whose names end with the cerastes is shewn by an inscription in one of the tombs near the Pyramids of El-Geezeh to have been contemporary with a personage who lived during, or shortly after, the time of Num-shufu; and in another inscription, in the tomb of a personage who lived in the time of Shaf-ra, also near the same Pyramids, the same King is mentioned with Shaf-ra, Men-kau-ra, U-seser-kef, and a King whom I believe to be Shura; the five names being placed side by side*. It is therefore perfectly evident that the name is that of a Thinite King who reigned soon after

the commencement of the Fourth and Fifth Dynasties; and I can have no doubt of its being that of Manetho's " Tlas." The reading of the hieroglyphic name is doubtful: if " Tlas " be not a corruption, it may possibly read " Telea-ses-kef," as the first character, which is a sitting figure or statue, is the only one which is doubtful, and ⲦⲈⲖⲈⲖ is a Coptic word, signifying "forma" and the like.—The account of the Fourth and Fifth Dynasties, soon to be given, and the table of the hieroglyphic names of Kings at the end of the volume, will explain what I have here said of the Memphites

* See Plate IV., No. 4.

Sect. III.]   SECOND DYNASTY.   107

and Elephantinites.—The name of "Sethenês" in the Tablet of Abydos is partly erased, and is as follows:

that of his successor, the "Chairês" of Manetho, is Men-ka-ra.

In the reign of Nephercherês, (or Nufre-ka-ra,)

the seventh King of the Second Dynasty, we are told that it was fabled that the Nile flowed mixed with honey for the space of eleven days. Manetho, if his very words on this subject are preserved, qualifies this statement; merely giving it on the authority of tradition. The next King, Sesôchris, (perhaps Snufre-ka,) was said, we are told, to have been a man of gigantic stature. According to Africanus's version of Manetho's lists, the Thinite Kingdom lasted five hundred and fifty-five years; and according to Eusebius's, five hundred and forty-nine; and according to the former version, Chenerês (Ka-en-ra)

was the last King. Both versions are shewn to be erroneous by the Tablet of Abydos; from which we learn that ten Kings reigned after Chenerês, and that the duration of the Second Dynasty was most probably little less than four hundred years.

I have already shewn that, according to my scheme of Egyptian Chronology, the Memphite Kingdom commenced shortly after the Thinite. In Manetho's list, we are told that in the reign of Necherôphês, or Necherôchis, the first King of the Third, which was the first Memphite, Dynasty, the Libyans revolted from the Egyptians, but returned to their allegiance, being terrified by a sudden increase of the moon. It is scarcely necessary to remark, that an optical illusion is evidently here intended; but the statement that the Libyans were at this early period subject to the Egyptians is very interesting, as shewing what importance Egypt had then acquired. The second King of Memphis, Tosorthros, or Sesorthos, is said in the lists to have been called by the Egyptians Æsculapius, on account of his medical knowledge, and to have invented the art of building with hewn stones, and to have patronized literature. In this passage, the Greek text of Eusebius has a vague term, (οἰκοδομὴν,) instead of the plainer term οἰκοδομίαν; but the rest of the sentence, as well as the testimony of the Armenian translation, shews that Africanus's reading is the better one. It is worthy of remark that the Tower of Babel was built of brick. Several of the names of the Kings of this Dynasty have been thought to be recognised on the monuments.

The next Memphite Dynasty was the Fourth, some of the Kings of which possessed great power, and made themselves famous by the wonderful monuments which they raised. At this period of Egyptian history, we begin to be able to study the chronicles of the early Kings from contemporary records; and as this is the time at which we can first decidedly ascribe certain Pyramids to particular Kings, it will not be amiss to controvert an opinion which has gained some adherents. It has been supposed that each Pyramid was the tomb of a sovereign or sovereigns, and that all the Pyramids were built before the Shepherd-invasion, being the tombs of successive Kings. It is enough to remark that ancient authority, the evidence of the monuments, and the relative positions of Pyramids, are against this theory; and the monuments distinctly shew that contemporaneous Kings were buried in the Pyramids around Memphis. Under these circumstances, it is manifestly unnecessary to enter upon this question in detail; and I have merely mentioned it to warn the reader against accepting as facts unsupported hypotheses, however boldly put forth.

According to the scheme of the Dynasties which I have adopted, the Fifth Dynasty (of Elephantinites) was, in its earlier part, contemporary with the Fourth (of Memphites); and the records in the tombs at the Pyramids satisfactorily prove this to have been the case.

Certain names, which can only be those of Elephantinites of the Fifth Dynasty, are found in tombs at the Pyramids of the time of the Fourth Dynasty; and, in these instances, are mentioned with Kings of that

Dynasty. Consequently, we must conclude that they were contemporary with these Memphite Kings; for they could not have been anterior to them. In order to render what I have to say on this subject more intelligible than it would be otherwise, I subjoin a table of the Fourth Dynasty and part of the Fifth.

FOURTH DYNASTY.

MANETHO.		MONUMENTS.
1. Sôris	29	Shura, or Khura.
2. Sûphis	63 ⎫	Shufu, or Khufu.
3. Sûphis.	66 ⎭	Num-shufu, or Num-khufu.
4. Mencherês	63	Men-kau-ra.
5. Ratoisês	25	
6. Bicherês	22	
7. Sebercherês	7	
8. Thamphthis	9	

PART OF THE FIFTH DYNASTY.

MANETHO.		MONUMENTS.
1. Usercherês	28	U-seser-kef.
2. Sephrês	13	Shaf-ra.
3. Nephercherês	20	Nufr-ar-ka-ra.
4. Sisirês	7	Seser-en-ra.

It will be seen in a later part of this work, that the last three Kings of the Fifth Dynasty in Africanus's version, and in the Royal Turin Papyrus, are separated from the earlier Kings, whose names are found at the Pyramids, by a very long interval of time; and that Eusebius's number of thirty-one Kings is more accurate than Africanus's of eight or nine, and is probably the true number. It is not certain whether Rathurês and Cherês belonged to the earlier or the later part of the Dynasty.

In one of the tombs near the Pyramids of El-Geezeh we find many royal names, some of which belong to the Fourth Dynasty, and some to the Fifth. The tomb is that which Champollion calls that of Eimaï, one of the principal persons buried in it, an officer of Sûphis I.; and in one of its chambers we find a kind of list of Kings, which contains the names of two Memphites, and one Elephantinite, in the following order: Shura; Num-shufu; Num-shufu; Nufr-ar-ka-ra*; and in another part of the same tomb we find a similar list, with the names of two Elephantinites and one Memphite, thus: Nufr-ar-ka-ra; Shura; Seser-en-ra†. The only peculiarities in these lists is the repetition of the name of Num-shufu in the first of them.

The reason for the manner in which these lists are arranged seems to me to be obvious. The first indicates that Nufr-ar-ka-ra was partly contemporary with Shura, and partly with Num-shufu; and the second, that Shura was partly contemporary with Nufr-ar-ka-ra. There are two Kings in Manetho's lists to whom Nufr-ar-ka-ra might be supposed to correspond, besides the Elephantinite Nephercherês; namely, Nephercherês, the seventh King of the Second Dynasty, of Thinites, and Sebercherês, supposed by some to be a copyist's mistake for Nephercherês, the seventh King of the Fourth Dynasty, of Memphites. Neither of these Kings, however, can be Nufr-ar-ka-ra; for the former is recognised in the Tablet of Abydos, and the latter is too long after the Sûphises to be mentioned in the tomb in which these lists occur. Further, we find traces of Elephantinite race in the names of the Kings of the Fourth Dynasty; for in the name of Num-shufu, the first syllable, Num, or Nev, is the name of the tutelary god of Elephantine; and we cannot fail

* Plate IV., No. 3.   † Plate IV., No. 2.

to observe similarities in the names of the Memphites and Elephantinites as found in the lists of Manetho, and on the monuments. From these considerations it appears that the Elephantinites of the Fifth Dynasty were contemporary with the Memphites of the Fourth. Some suppose that the Fifth Dynasty ruled at Memphis after the Fourth. This hypothesis, however, I have sufficiently disproved; but I shall also have to mention a fact relating to the latter part of the Fifth Dynasty which would be conclusive on this point by itself if we had no other evidence. But there is an objection which may be urged against the manner in which I have stated certain Kings of the Fourth and Fifth Dynasties to have been contemporary. If the monuments show Sôris to have been partly contemporary with Nufr-ar-ka-ra, how are we to explain the fact of Manetho's making the reigns of the predecessors of Nephercherês to have been twelve years longer than that of Sôris, unless we suppose that the Fifth Dynasty commenced a little before the Fourth, which is unlikely? But we must remember that Manetho's numbers are incorrect as they now stand in many places, and that he reckons co-regent Kings as if in succession.

I have mentioned another very important record, in which five Kings' names are placed side by side in a tomb near the Pyramids of El-Geezeh. They are Shaf-ra, Men-kau-ra, the King who appears to be the Thinite Tlas of Manetho, U-seser-kef, and a much erased name which is apparently Shura. (See Plate IV., No. 4.) This is another strong proof of the contemporaneousness of the Memphites and Elephantinites. I am indebted to the kindness of Mrs. Lieder for a copy of this valuable record.

The name of Sôris, the first King of the Fourth

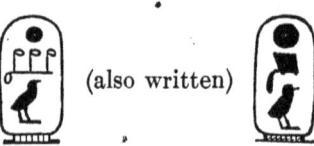

(also written)

Dynasty, is, as I have already remarked, found in the tombs near the Pyramids, and reads "Shura." His name was also found, by Mr. Perring, in the quarry-marks of the Northern Pyramid of Aboo-Seer, in the Memphite Necropolis; and hence it appears that this was his tomb. We know nothing of the history of his reign, nor of that of Usercherês, the first King of the Fifth Dynasty, who reigned about the same time, and whose name, which reads U-seser-kef, I here give.

The second King of the Fifth Dynasty is called by Manetho, according to Africanus, Sephrês. This can only be Shaf-ra, or Khaf-ra, whose name is found in many of the tombs near the Pyramids of El-

Geezeh. Herodotus and Diodorus Siculus call him, respectively, Chephrên, and Kephrên; and ascribe to him the building of " the Second Pyramid."* Both these authors call him the brother and successor of the builder of the Great Pyramid, whom the former calls Cheops; and the latter, Chembês, or Chemmis, the Khufu, or Shufu, of the monuments, and Sûphis I. of Manetho. Diodorus adds that some said he was the son of Chembês, by name Chabryïs, that is, Khafra; and both historians assign to Chephrên, or Kephrên, a reign of fifty-six years. In the inscriptions of his own time, Shafra repeatedly receives a title which some have read " Shafra of the Little Pyramid," and which, however it is interpreted, must be understood as connecting him with a Pyramid. Manetho assigns to him a reign of only thirteen years, and from what I have said above respecting the first three Kings of the Fifth Dynasty it seems that this is not less than the true duration of his reign. Notwithstanding this, the Second Pyramid is the largest of all the Pyramids, excepting the Great Pyramid. How are we to account for these apparent discrepancies? The Second Pyramid, which cannot be doubted for a moment to have been founded by Shafra, presents peculiarities which explain this difficulty. I subjoin a section of it.

* That Shaf-ra is Chephrên is an opinion which has been held by my uncle (Mr. E. W. Lane) for many years; and probably by several others.

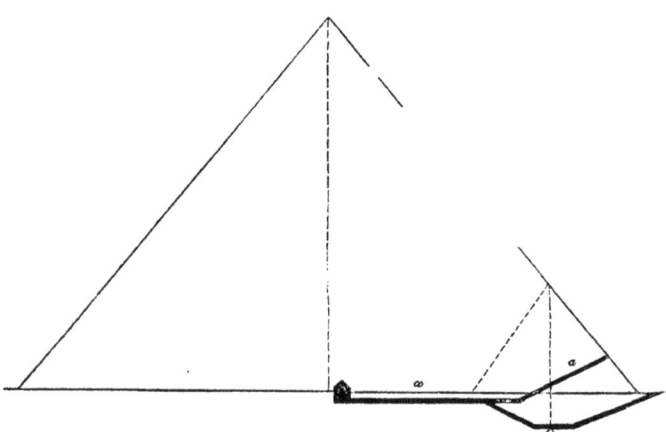

The peculiarities of this Pyramid will be understood by comparing it with others. In general we find that a Pyramid has but one entrance, and one sepulchral chamber; but there are some exceptions to this rule; and of these exceptions, the Second Pyramid is one of the most remarkable. It seems that Shafra built a small Pyramid over the northern chamber; and that a later King founded another Pyramid over the southern chamber, and continued to enlarge it until it included that of Shafra. Herodotus and Diodorus place Chephrên (or Shafra) between the builders of the First and Third Pyramids, probably because of the position of his Pyramid; and with respect to his relationship to Cheops, or Chemmis, what these historians say on that subject we may reasonably suppose to have arisen from the fact that the Fourth and Fifth Dynasties were contemporary, and perhaps even consisted of princes of one family. It might be supposed to be unlikely that an Elephantinite King should be buried at Memphis; but Mr. Perring has found the name of another Elephantinite King, Seser-en-ra, among quarry-marks on a part of one of the Pyramids of Aboo-Seer; and we also find the names of Elephantinite Kings in tombs near the Pyramids of El-Geezeh. Memphis, it is well known, was a sacred city, and one of the reputed burial-places of Osiris.

The third King of the Fifth Dynasty is called by Manetho Nephercherês, and on the monuments, Nufr-ar-ka-ra, as I have already shown. All we know

respecting him is, that he appears to have been partly contemporary with Shura, or Sôris, after whom,

Manetho, according to the transcript of Africanus, mentions two Kings of the name of Sûphis; Sûphis I., the second King, and Sûphis II., the third King, of the Fourth Dynasty. These two Kings correspond to the Shufu, or Khufu[1], and Num-shufu, or Num-khufu[2],

1   2

of the monuments. I formerly supposed that these two names applied to one King, the Sûphis I. of Manetho's list of the Fourth Dynasty, as given by Africanus. My reasons were, that both names occur in the quarry-marks on the stones of the Great Pyramid (see Col. Vyse's Pyramids), and that a personage buried in a tomb at the Pyramids mentions Shufu in its inscriptions, and in the same tomb has employed a stone of another building of his own, containing a record of the commencement of the Second G. P. Y. in an inscription of the time of Num-shufu. I believed this to be confirmed by the statement of Manetho, according to Eusebius, that Sûphis I., who built the greatest Pyramid, "was arrogant towards the Gods; but, repenting, wrote the sacred book, which the Egyptians esteem as a great treasure." (In Africanus's version we read that "he was also arrogant towards the gods, and he wrote the sacred book," &c.; implying, though not directly stating, his repentance.) For I found that Num-shufu, which I believed to be the first name of Sûphis I. for a reason already stated, was a name which seemed to indicate the arrogancy of Sûphis towards the gods, as Num-shufu signifies " Num (or Kneph) the long-haired ; " and I concluded that, on his repentance, Sûphis I. assumed a common appellation, Shufu, "the long-haired." This etymology we owe to the ingenuity of the learned Rosellini. (Monumenti Storici, T. i., p. 128.) I added that, although almost all the names of Egyptian monarchs, handed down to us by the monuments, are partly composed of the names of gods, they may (as far as I am aware) be divided into two classes, neither of which comprehends such a name as Num-shufu. Lastly, the opinion above mentioned I more readily adopted on finding that a friend, upon whose judgment I place great reliance, and with whom I discussed this point in Cairo, agreed with me in believing the two names in question to apply to one King.

This opinion I must now retract; for my friend, the

Reverend Mr. Lieder (to whom I am very deeply indebted for his having supplied me with very valuable materials, as well as for much learned criticism upon this and other subjects treated in the first edition of this essay, and for most important aid which he has rendered me in every branch of my studies during a long course of years), has informed me that he has lately found both the names in question upon the monument which contains the inverted block. Hence I conclude that Shufu is Sûphis I.; and Num-shufu, Sûphis II.; and I believe them to have reigned together, from the manner in which they are here mentioned, and from their names being found in the Great Pyramid, which has two great chambers, and which all are agreed in stating to have been built in the reign of one King. My reason for identifying Shufu with Sûphis I. is, that Shufu is evidently the correct name of the King to whom Herodotus ascribes the building of the Great Pyramid, which Manetho ascribes to Sûphis I.

Herodotus calls the King who built the Great Pyramid "Cheops," that is Khufu, a manner of pronouncing Shufu; and he tells us of his impiety and cruelty, assigning to him a reign of fifty years. Diodorus calls him "Chembês," or "Chemmis;" and likewise gives him a reign of fifty years. ("Chembês" is evidently a corruption of Khufu.) He also tells us that, from the erection of the Great Pyramid to his time, not less than a thousand years, or as some wrote, more than three thousand and four hundred years, had elapsed. Both these statements are manifestly incorrect. The other statements of these historians respecting this King and the Great Pyramid are well known, and this is not the place to discuss them, as they do not furnish any important contributions to our knowledge of general Egyptian history.

The reign of Sûphis I. is stated by Manetho to have lasted sixty-three, and that of Sûphis II., sixty-six, years. From this it appears that the two Kings reigned sixty-three years together, and that Sûphis II. reigned three years after the close of the reign of Sûphis I.; or perhaps they were not so long co-regents, and the reign of Sûphis II. may have lasted a few years more than three after his predecessor's had concluded: but however this may be, it is certain that the approximative chronology of this Dynasty derived from dates of the Calendar of the Panegyries, &c., plainly shows that there is an errour of about sixty years in this part of Manetho's list, as preserved by Africanus.

I have already mentioned the date of the commencement of the second Great Panegyrical Year, B.C. 2352, in the time of the two Sûphises. The interval from Mênês to Sûphis I. remarkably agrees with the interval of one Great Panegyrical Year from the Era of Menes to the date of the Sûphises: for the Third Dynasty evidently commenced during, or soon after, the reign of Athôthis, the successor of Mênês, and therefore the whole interval from the Era of Mênês to the accession of Sûphis I. could not much exceed the sum of the reigns of Mênês and Athôthis, with the length of the Third Dynasty, and of the reign of Sôris. According to Africanus, this sum is 362 years; and according to Eusebius, it is probably less. This I regard as a remarkable confirmation of the chronological system put forth in Part I., when we consider that Manetho's lists have, in so many instances, errours in excess.

From what I have already remarked respecting the Kings of the Fourth and Fifth Dynasties, it appears that Sisirês, the fourth King of the latter Dynasty, whose hieroglyphic name is Seser-en-ra, was contempo-

rary with the two Sûphises. Mr. Perring, who is well known for the ability and success with which he continued Colonel Vyse's researches at the Pyramids, found this King's name, or rather a variation of it, in the quarry-marks of the Middle Pyramid of Aboo-Seer, which was therefore most probably built by him.

The fourth King of the Fourth Dynasty, the successor of Sûphis II., is called by Manetho, according to Africanus, " Mencherês." This is the same King whom

Herodotus and Diodorus call " Mykerinos;" the latter writer adding, that some call him "Mecherinos." To him they ascribe the erection of the Third Pyramid; and Colonel Vyse found his hieroglyphic name, Men-kaù-ra, on part of his mummy-case when he opened that Pyramid. In Manetho's list of the Dynasties, as given by Africanus and Eusebius, the building of this Pyramid is attributed to Queen Nitôkris, the last sovereign of the Sixth Dynasty, though Eusebius's version seems to state this merely on the authority of tradition. It will be seen by consulting the plans and sections in Colonel Vyse's excellent work on the Pyramids, that the Third Pyramid was originally much smaller than it is at present: it appears that Queen Nitôkris enlarged it, and made a new passage in the rock beneath it, leading to a new chamber: thus the original entrance is found to be at a considerable distance within the face of the Pyramid.

The names of the successors of Mencherês in the Fourth Dynasty are not, as far as I know, found upon the monuments. The same is the case with respect to the Kings whom Africanus's list makes the fifth and sixth Kings of the Fifth Dynasty; but the names of the last three Kings of that Dynasty are found together in the Royal Turin Papyrus, and the name and square-title of the last are also found in hieroglyphic inscriptions. These names, which I give in the hieroglyphic characters corresponding to the hieratic of the Papyrus, I now subjoin, with the lengths of their reigns from the Royal Papyrus and Manetho (Afr.).

Men-ka-hor, 8 years.   Tet. . . 28 years.   Unas, 30 years.
Mencherês, 9   ,,   Tancherês, 44 ,,   Onnos, 33 ,,

Perhaps these differences in the lengths of reigns, as stated in the Royal Papyrus and by Manetho, may be thus explained. As we do not know the number of months, the eight years of the Papyrus probably correspond to the nine which Manetho assigns to Mencherês; the real sum having doubtless been eight years and some months. The length of the reign of Tancherês in Manetho is probably a repetition of that of Rhathurês. In the case of Onnos we cannot be sure that the units have not dropped out in the Papyrus; so that Manetho's thirty-three years may be the correct sum.

While writing this work, I have received from my friend, the Reverend Mr. Lieder, one of the most important of all the evidences that I now possess of the correctness of my scheme of the order of the Dynasties. In a letter to me from Cairo, he has informed me that he has found, by clearing out a remarkable tomb near the Great Pyramid, of the time of Assa, the fifth Shepherd-King of the Fifteenth Dynasty, the names of Unas and Assa together, in an inscription in that tomb; remarking that they belonged to the same Dynasty, one being the predecessor of the other, or were contemporary. After the receipt of the communication above-mentioned, another letter brought me a copy of the inscription in which the two Kings are mentioned together, and of another containing the name of Assa; each drawn by Mrs. Lieder, on a large scale, and evidently with the most scrupulous accuracy, with illustrative remarks by Mr. Lieder. The tomb, which is that of a high functionary named Snemt-em-hat, as his name most probably reads, is near the north-west angle of the Great Pyramid. I give a copy of the inscription containing the two names in Plate V.

This important inscription is divided into three parts: —first, the record of the celebration of Panegyries, which, not containing any date, excepting that of " the beginning of the year," I do not give: secondly, two lateral inscriptions, each composed of the titles of Snemt-em-hat, who is called "devoted to Assa," and "devoted to Unas;" thus standing in the same relation to both Kings. In the lines in which Unas and Assa are both mentioned, Unas is called " Lord of Upper and Lower Egypt," while both he and Assa receive no titles in the other cases in which they are mentioned in the same inscription. This shows plainly that Unas, the last

King of the Fifth Dynasty, was contemporary with Assa, the fifth King of the Fifteenth; and hence we may make two very important deductions:—first, that the Elephantinites did not reign at Memphis between the Fourth and Sixth Dynasties; secondly, if we calculate average Kings' reigns in the table of the hieroglyphic names of the Kings of the first seventeen Dynasties, from the commencement of the Fourth Dynasty to the reign of Assa, the result will show that Eusebius's sum of thirty-one Kings of the Fifth Dynasty is, at least, very near the truth. The sums of the Fourth and Sixth Dynasties, and of the Fifteenth, excluding the reign of the last King, is about 577 years, which would give an average of about eighteen years for the reign of each King of the Fifth Dynasty, supposing that Dynasty to have consisted of thirty-one Kings. The contemporaneousness of Unas and Assa thus proved on monumental evidence is of the greatest importance, since it is one of the proofs of the contemporaneousness, in the manner which I have already explained, of the Kingdoms of the Fifth and Fifteenth Dynasties, and those between them; five out of the seven columns of the table of contemporary Dynasties being thus satisfactorily shown to be correct by this one evidence; in addition to which there is also a variety of evidence, already adduced, by which the correctness of the arrangement of the first two columns is proved. It seems to me to be probable that Assa treated Unas with respect, although doubtless more powerful himself, from motives of policy, as the latter was a legitimate Egyptian King.

Before continuing this investigation in order, it is necessary to consider the monumental lists of those Dynasties whose history I am about to examine; and I trust that the reader will excuse the dryness of some of the preliminary details which I place before him in order to present to him a complete view of the data by which I am guided in this inquiry. The most important of the monumental data is the list of Kings commonly called that of "the Chamber of Kings."

This list was sculptured in a small chamber of the great temple of El-Karnak, and is now in the Louvre, to which collection it was presented by M. Prisse, who removed it from Egypt. It contained sixty-one royal rings, fifteen of which are entirely obliterated, and ten much injured; the remaining thirty-six being perfect, or nearly so. I shall now show in what order this list was arranged, and how the monuments enable us to ascertain that order.

The list is divided into two equal parts; one containing originally thirty, and the other thirty-one, royal names, arranged in four rows: that part containing thirty-one names, and which was to the left of a person entering the chamber, is universally allowed to contain the names of sovereigns of whom some, at least, were anterior to those of the other part. This part, therefore, I now examine.

The lowest line reads from right to left, as is proved by our finding that No. 5, Seser-en-ra, whose prenomen is composed of the same signs as those of the name of an earlier King, (Sisirês,) differently disposed, was a predecessor of No. 8, Ter-ka-ra (Sesertesen I.); and further, that No. 7, Sken-en-ra, was the immediate predecessor of the same King*. The second line, or that immediately above this, reads from left to right; as No. 9, Amenemha I., reigned conjointly with No. 8,

* Colonel Felix's Notes on Hieroglyphics.

Sesertesen I.; and as Nos. 10, 11, 12, and 13, were his successors; for although the names of Nos. 10 and 13 alone remain, their relative positions render this certain. The next, or third line from the bottom, reads in the same manner, that is, from left to right; for No. 22, Papa, is placed as the immediate predecessor of No. 23, Mer-en-ra, in a list, thrice occurring, in the grottoes of Chenoboscion. The fourth and last line of the same compartment also reads in the same manner; for No. 25, Snufre, was the successor of Nufre-ka-ra, as we learn from the Turin Royal Papyrus; and Nufre-ka-ra in the Chenoboscion lists immediately succeeds No. 23, Mer-en-ra. These are sufficient proofs of the correctness of my arrangement of each line of this side of the list; and I am convinced that the lowest line is the first, and that the lines above it regularly continue the list; the next being the second; that above it, the third; and the uppermost, the fourth; on the following evidence:—In the first line, No. 8 is the first King of a Dynasty, other Kings of which are found in the next line. In the second line, No. 15, Nantef I., is the first King of a Dynasty, which is continued in the line above. Lastly, in the third line we find Kings which in the lists of Chenoboscion precede the first King of a Dynasty, other Kings of which are found in the fourth line. It will be seen that these views are amply confirmed by the monuments, by Manetho, and by the Turin Royal Papyrus.

To render my explanation of this most important record more clear, I here insert the names in Roman characters, in the order in which they are there arranged, giving both parts of the list*.

* For the Hieroglyphic names, see Plate VI.

LIST OF THE CHAMBER OF KINGS, [Part II.

39.	47.		
38. Sha-nufre-ra.	46. Mee-hem-ra.	54. Wah-shau-ra.	61. ...ra.
37. Sha-hem-ra.	45. Mee-kau-ra.	53. Swah-en-ra.	60. Snuf-re-...ra.
36.	44. Seser-tete-ra.	52. Mee-hotp-ra.	59. S...en-ra.
35. Hem-Khu-tete-ra.	43. ...ra.	51. Khu-tete-ra.	58. Hem-..tete-ra.
34. Sankh-hat-ra.	42. Snufre-...ra.	50.	57.
33. S...en.	41. Sha-...ra.	49.	56.
32.	40. Sha-ankh-ra.	48. Hem-..shau-ra.	55.
31. Hem-smen-tete-ra.	23. Mer-en-ra.	15. Nan-tef.	1. ...ra.
30.	22. [Pa]pa.	14. Ra-sebak-nufre.	2. Snufre-ka-ra.
29.	21. [Tata.]	13. Ma-tu-ra.	3. Neb-tu-ra.
28. Ass.	20. Na[ntef.]	12.	4. Nub-ter-ra.
27. A-an.	19. Mun[t-hotp.]	11.	5. Seser-en-ra.
26. Shura.	18. Nan[tef.]	10. Nub-kau-ra.	6. Snecht-en-ra.
25. S-nufre.	17. Nantef.	9. S-hotp-[hat-] ra.	7. Sken-en-ra.
24.	16. [Nantef. naä.]		8. Ter-ka-ra.

Another tabular view which I insert will, I hope, render what I have to say still more plain. It will be seen that the Eleventh and Twelfth Dynasties are placed first: then the Ninth, Sixth, and Fifteenth, because contemporary with the Eleventh and Twelfth; and then the Thirteenth. The first column contains the nomen or prenomen from the left part of the list in Roman characters; for in some cases the nomen is given, in others, the prenomen. When the other name of a King, whether it be nomen or prenomen, is found on the monuments or in the Royal Turin Papyrus, I have inserted it in brackets; and where the name is partially erased in the table, I have been sometimes able to restore it from these authorities. The second column contains corroborations of the arrangement from the list of Kings called the Tablet of Abydos, and from the Lists of Chenoboscion; these extracts being distinguished by the abbreviations T. A. and L. C. The third column contains parts of the Royal Turin Papyrus corresponding to the List of the Chamber of Kings; and the fourth contains the portions of Manetho's List (according to the transcript of Africanus) which correspond to this List. The extracts from the Papyrus relating to the Twelfth Dynasty will be found more fully given in a table in page 156.

128   TABLE OF LISTS OF KINGS.   [Par

I. Chamber of Kings.		II. Tab. Abyd., etc.	III. Turin Papyrus.	IV. Manetho.	
	Nomens.	Names.	Names.	Name.	Yrs.
.... ra.					
Snufre-ka-ra.					
Neb-tu-ra.					
Nub-ter-ra.					
Seser-en-ra.					
Snekht-en-ra.					
Sken- n-ra.					
Ter-ka-ra.				Sesonchôsis.	
S-hotp-[hat]-ra.	[Sesertesen I.]		.	nhês.	
Nub-kau-ra.	[Amenemha I.]	Nub-kau-ra. T. A.	.	nhês.	
	[Amenemha II.]	Sha-ter-ra. T. A.	.	Sesôstris.	
		Sha-kau-ra. T. A.	.	Lacharês.	
		Ma-en-ra. T. A.	.	Amerês.	
Ma-tu-ra.		Ma-tu-ra. T. A.	Ma-tu-ra	Amenemês.	
Ra-sebak-nufre.			Ra-sebak-nufre	Skemiophris.	
				Achthoês.	
[. . ap.-ma-ra.]	Nantef [I.]				
	[Nantef (II.) Nau.]				
	Nantef [III.]			40ês.	
[. . her-hep-ma-ra.]	Nan[tef IV.]			Phiôps.	
f te-ra.]	(t-hotp.)			Menthesûphis.	
	Na[ntef V.?]			Nitôkris.	
] M-ra.]	[Tata.]	Mee-ra. Papa. L. C.	Netakartee	Saitês.	
M- n-ra.	Papa.	Mer-en-ra. L. C.	Nufre-ka.	Bnôn.	
[Nufre-ka-ra?]		Nufre-ka-ra. L. C.	Snufre.	Pachnan.	
Snufre.	[Pi-ankhee]		Ab....	Staan (Iannas,)	
Shura.	[Ab ....]			Archlês (Assis.)	
	A-an.			Apôbis (Apôphis.)	
[Tet-ka-ra]	Ass.				

I must now proceed to show the evidence of the contemporaneousness and relative rank of these Kings, from the titles here given to them, which are very various, and are evidently disposed, not ornamentally nor regularly, but generally according to the rank of the Dynasty or King. In the first place we observe, that the twelve remaining of the first fourteen names are prenomens; and that, of the other names, twelve in number, exclusive of the five erased rings, only three are prenomens, all the rest being nomens, although other monuments give us the prenomens of many of them. Secondly, the first fourteen Kings have all similar titles, as far as those titles are preserved, " Lord of all Egypt," " Lord of Upper and Lower Egypt," " Good God," and " Lord aree-khet," a title of which the signification is uncertain. No. 15, Nantef I., has the title " Good God, lord of Upper and Lower Egypt." Nos. 17, 18, 19, are each called " Horus," or " Prince ;" and their second title is, in each case, almost, or wholly, effaced. No. 20 is merely called " Chief." No. 22, Papa, and No. 23, Mer-en-ra, are both called " Lord of Upper and Lower Egypt." No. 25, Snufre, is called " Lord of all Egypt ;" and Nos. 26, 27, 28, only " Good God." Besides this, after every name is the title " Speaker of truth," in such a position supposed to signify "deceased." Hence it is evident that certain Kings are treated with much more honour than others, in this list. The reason is obvious: Thothmes III., who caused this record to be sculptured in the great temple of Thebes, was a Diospolite King, and therefore he gives prenomens to all the Kings of Diospolite Dynasties. The prenomen was undoubtedly more honourable than the nomen: the former being assumed by a King on his accession to the throne;

the latter being only a proper name. Thus the list is naturally divided into Diospolite Kings, and Kings contemporary with them. The latter Kings are again divided into Dynasties by their various titles. Are not these facts, I would ask, strongly confirmatory of the contemporaneousness of the early Dynasties? If the Dynasties contained in this list were all successive, how is it that their arrangement is totally different from that of Manetho? The arrangement is clear; for it cannot be denied that the left portion contains the Eleventh, Twelfth, part of the Ninth, the Sixth, and Fifteenth, Dynasties; only two of these Dynasties being successive in their numbers. In the Royal Turin Papyrus also, the Fifteenth Dynasty immediately follows the Sixth; the one concluding, and the other commencing, in the same fragment. These are strong evidences of contemporaneousness; but there is, in this list, a far stronger evidence, not only of the contemporaneousness of certain of the first seventeen Dynasties with others of the same portion of Manetho's list, but also of the particular scheme of contemporaneousness which I have adopted. The left portion of the list commences with the Eleventh and Twelfth Dynasties, and concludes with part of a Dynasty which is shown to be the Thirteenth, from the one name that remains; and I may here add, that I shall be able to show that all the Kings of the other, or right, half belong to the Thirteenth Dynasty. Therefore, the list commences with the Eleventh and Twelfth Dynasties, and concludes with the Thirteenth Dynasty; and therefore the intermediate Kings must be those who were for the most part contemporary with the Eleventh and Twelfth Dynasties. On referring to the table of contemporary Dynasties, it will be seen that the

Ninth, the Sixth, and the Fifteenth Dynasties were more or less contemporary with the Eleventh and Twelfth : thus

    6th - 9th - 11th.
             12th - 15th.
             13th.

I must now briefly state my reasons for assigning the Kings in this list to certain of Manetho's Dynasties. Nos. 8–14, inclusive, excepting No. 9, are the Kings of Manetho's Twelfth Dynasty: this is now so well proved that it cannot admit of the least doubt. The first seven Kings, since one of them is a direct ancestor, and another a predecessor, of the first King of the Twelfth Dynasty, must belong to the Eleventh Dynasty. No. 9, Amenemha I., is a King of the same Dynasty in Manetho's list; and is put after Sesertesen I., in the present list, probably because he reigned, for some part of his rule, conjointly with him. Nos. 15–20 are Kings of a Dynasty of which the third, fourth, and fifth Kings are called " Princes;" and the sixth is called " a Chief." I assign No. 15, Nantef I., to this Dynasty on account of his name, although his titles are different from those of his successors. After No. 20, one name is lost; and next we find the nomen of Mee-ra Papa, who corresponds to Phiôps, the fourth King of the Sixth Dynasty, in Africanus's version of Manetho's list; and the prenomen, Mer-en-ra, of his successor Menthesûphis immediately follows. We next find another name wanting; and then follow four names which are evidently those of the second, third, fourth, and fifth Kings of Manetho's Fifteenth Dynasty. Nos. 29 and 30 are erased. No. 31 is a King of the Thirteenth Dynasty, as I judge from his prenomen, which is similar to those of the Kings of that Dynasty which continue the list, and entirely occupy the right part, which I shall afterwards have to consider. As I have pointed out the Kings of the Sixth, Eleventh, Twelfth, and Fifteenth Dynasties, the Nantefs must be the earlier Kings of the Ninth. That they are of a Heracleopolite Dynasty is most satisfactorily proved by a fact which Sir Gardner Wilkinson has mentioned to me as a confirmation of my system, and therefore they can only be of the Ninth or Tenth Dynasty, the only two Heracleopolite Dynasties. Since certain of the Kings of the Nantef family are proved by the monuments to have been contemporary with the Eleventh Dynasty, as Munt-hotp was contemporary with Amenemha I., they can only be of the Ninth Dynasty.—On these evidences I have based the comparison between the list of Manetho and those of the monuments given in the preceding table. The most important differences in each Dynasty will be noticed in their proper places. The reader, however, will see at once that the Twelfth and Fifteenth Dynasties present no great difficulties. The Eleventh is shorter than in Manetho's list; a difference which is most probably caused by certain usurping Kings being included in that list, and excluded in this. The Sixth Dynasty contains two Kings too many in Manetho's list as given by Africanus: Queen Nitôkris is most probably here omitted, as it appears that the names of Queens were not generally admitted into the national lists; and in the lists of Chenoboscion we find Nufre-ka-ra, the prenomen of Salatis, placed immediately after Mer-en-ra; therefore his is most probably the wanting name, No. 24.

Respecting the other lists that I have adduced in confirmation of my arrangement of the list of the

Chamber of Kings, I have nothing to add to what I have already said, excepting with respect to the lists of Chenoboscion. A copy of one of these lists has been already published by Sir Gardner Wilkinson, who was the first to visit and describe the interesting tombs at that place. I have been enabled, by comparing these lists with the list of the Chamber of Kings and the Royal Turin Papyrus, to ascertain that Nufre-ka-ra, the last name at Chenoboscion, and probably the No. 24 of the list of the Chamber of Kings, is the prenomen of Salatis, the first Shepherd-King of the Fifteenth Dynasty. It is worthy of remark that the scribe who wrote the Royal Turin Papyrus omits the Ra in this prenomen, writing it Nufre-ka, as if to indicate that the King who bore it was a foreign King, and therefore not a Ra, or Pharaoh, by right. The solar disk, called " Ra," or " Phra " with the article, is the Egyptian for " Pharaoh," as is now acknowledged by all authorities.

I have now to resume my examination of that part of the history of Egypt which preceded the Shepherd-invasion, to which the remarks that I have been making form a necessary introduction.

The last Dynasties which I noticed were the Fourth, (Memphites,) and the Fifth, (Elephantinites,) which were partly contemporary, and therefore the next Dynasty to be considered is the Sixth, which immediately succeeded the Fourth, reigning at Memphis. To this Dynasty, Manetho, according to the transcript of Africanus, assigns six monarchs, and a duration of 203 years; the transcript of Eusebius also mentions the same duration, but does not state the number of monarchs. There is an evident errour in Africanus's list of this Dynasty. The second and third Kings,

Phios and Methusûphis, are repetitions of the fourth and fifth, Phiôps and Menthesûphis. My reasons for this assertion are, that but one King is wanting between a King of the Ninth Dynasty and Papa, in the list of the Chamber of Kings; that Sir Gardner Wilkinson has found the name of Phiôps with a King's name which he agrees with me in considering that of the first King of this Dynasty, and which cannot apply to either Phios or Methusûphis; and that the names of the two pairs of Kings are so remarkably similar. That Papa is Phiôps is quite certain from the length of the reign of that King in Manetho, and the monumental evidence in the numerous sculptures that he has left. We can therefore construct the following table of this Dynasty on the authority of Manetho and the monuments.

SIXTH DYNASTY.

MANETHO.		MONUMENTS.
1. Othoês 30		1. ——— Tata.
4. Phiôps 100		2. Mee-ra Papa.
5. Menthesûphis . . 1		3. Mer-en-ra ———.
6. Nitôkris 12		4. Neet-akartee.
Sum . . 143		

The hieroglyphic name of Othoês, the first King of this Dynasty, reads "Tata," but it was also pronounced

"Atat" or "Athath," as "Papa" was pronounced "Apap" or "Aphaph." In Manetho's lists we read that Othoês

was slain by his guards. We know nothing more respecting him.

We are also told in Manetho's lists that Phiôps began to reign when he was six years old. His hieroglyphic name is found in many tablets and inscriptions

in various parts of Egypt, which show that he was a very powerful King. I have already noticed the circumstance of his having left many records of the celebration of the commencements of periods of Royal Panegyries, or Jubilees; affording a strong confirmation of the long reign which Manetho assigns to him; for if the Jubilee in the thirtieth or thirty-first year of a King's reign were remarkable, how much more remarkable must have been that in his sixtieth or sixty-first year, and still more so that in his ninetieth or ninety-first year.

We know nothing respecting the successor of Phiôps, who is called in Africanus's list Menthesûphis, but that his prenomen was Mer-en-ra.

Queen Nitôkris concluded the Sixth Dynasty, according to Manetho, in Africanus's version, and according to the Royal Turin Papyrus. I give her name, rendered into hieroglyphics, from the hieratic characters of that record. In Manetho's list we are told that she built the Third Pyramid, a statement which I

have already had occasion to notice in treating of the Fourth Dynasty. Herodotus also mentions Queen Nitôkris. With her the Sixth Dynasty ended; the Shepherds, who had lately invaded Egypt, taking Memphis, which they continued to hold for more than two centuries. I shall have to speak of the invasion of Egypt by the Shepherds, and their domination, in the next section.

During the Sixth Dynasty, the Heracleopolite kingdom commenced; and its first Dynasty was the Ninth. Of the Kings of this Dynasty, Manetho's lists mention but one, the first, by name; but the hieroglyphic names of several of them have been ascertained by me. I have already mentioned the fact of Sir Gardner Wilkinson's having found a proof that the Kings of the Nantef family found in the Chamber of Kings are Kings of a Heracleopolite Dynasty: it is this: five of the six Kings of the Nantef family have nomens into the composition of which the name of the Egyptian Hercules, the god of Sebennytus, and also doubtless of Heracleopolis, enters; and this proves that these six Kings belong to a Heracleopolite Dynasty, which can only be the Ninth, for I have already shown that it cannot be the Tenth. This fact is even of greater importance than it appears to be at first sight; for it not only proves that the Kings whose names are Nos.

15–20, inclusive, in the list of the Chamber of Kings, are of Manetho's Ninth Dynasty, but it also furnishes one of the many proofs of the contemporaneousness of certain of Manetho's Dynasties. It is so evident from the monuments that the Nantefs were immediately before the Twelfth Dynasty, that Mr. Birch and M. de Rougé concluded they must be of the Eleventh Dynasty. Even if they were right in this, which I have shown could not be the case, the proof of contemporaneousness would not be in the least invalidated, since two of the Kings of the true Eleventh Dynasty are shown by their relationship and connection with Sesertesen I. to have been contemporaries of the Nantefs; not to mention the direct proofs of contemporaneousness.

Six names of Kings of the Ninth Dynasty are given in the list of the Chamber of Kings, while Manetho, according to Africanus, assigns to it nineteen Kings, and according to Eusebius, four. The latter number is obviously erroneous, so that Africanus's is probably right, since it is not likely that both are wrong. How is it, then, that only six names are given in the list of the Chamber of Kings? The last Nantef whose name is given in the Chamber of Kings is called merely "chief," and I shall be able to show that he reigned about the time of the commencement of the Twelfth Dynasty; and this shows, apparently, why none of his successors are given in this list; for the Twelfth Dynasty may be supposed, with great probability, from this, to have laid claim to the dominions of the Heracleopolites; and it is evident that the Diospolites of the Eleventh Dynasty were as inferior in power to the earlier Heracleopolites as the later Heracleopolites were to the Diospolites of the Twelfth, and afterwards to the Shepherds. Respecting the Chronology of the Heracleopolite kingdom, it appears to me that it is not very difficult to form a tolerably accurate judgment. If we take the durations that Africanus assigns to the Ninth and Tenth Dynasties, the whole sum is thirty-eight Kings who reigned five hundred and ninety-four years. I have already shown the probability that Africanus is correct with respect to the Ninth Dynasty; and I must remark that the number of Kings is agreeable with the length he assigns to it. With respect to the Tenth Dynasty, Africanus and Eusebius entirely agree in the number of its Kings, and the duration of their rule. Most probably this Dynasty ended at the time of the great Shepherd-war of expulsion. I subjoin a table of the two Dynasties, from Manetho, according to Africanus, and from the monuments.

NINTH DYNASTY.

MANETHO.	MONUMENTS.
1. Achthoês	1. Nantef [I.]
(2)	2. Nantef [II.] Naä.
(3)	3. Nantef [III.]
(4)	4. Nantef [IV.] ....
(5)	5. Munt-hotp.
(6)	6. Na[ntef V.]
Thirteen more Kings.	

TENTH DYNASTY.
Nineteen Kings.

Manetho, according to the lists, tells us that Achthoês was more cruel than any of his predecessors, and did evil to all the Egyptians; and, at last, was seized with madness, and killed by a crocodile. It is well known that in some parts of Egypt the crocodile was particularly venerated; and in others, execrated and destroyed; and among those who were most noted for their hostility to that animal were the Heracleopolites*. Was Achthoês a warlike King, who gained considerable power in Upper Egypt, and ruled in his own nome with lenity, and in other parts of his kingdom with severity; and in consequence did some of the ancient Egyptians execrate, and others revere, the animal that killed him? The reader may remember the tradition related by Diodorus Siculus †, respecting the preservation of an ancient King by a crocodile. The learned Sir Gardner Wilkinson remarks, that, although Diodorus calls the King so preserved " Mènas" (his mode of writing Mênês), the story evidently refers to Mœris, from what follows it ‡. It appears that the hieroglyphic nomen of Achthoês is Nantef; the former name is probably his prenomen. In the list of the Chamber of Kings, Nantef I.'s nomen is written thus:

his prenomen is not yet found, as far as I am aware. The name Nantef is also written more fully:

 and abbreviated thus:

---

* In speaking of Heracleopolis, I mean the city of that name in Middle Egypt, which, without doubt, was the city of the Kings of the Ninth and Tenth Dynasties.

† I. 89.   ‡ Ancient Egyptians, Second Series, vol. ii., p. 233.

I have found the nomen of Nantef III. written with the former of these variations.

The nomen, prenomen, and square title, of Nantef II., surnamed "the Great," have been found in hieroglyphics. There is satisfactory evidence, which is

known to Sir Gardner Wilkinson and Mr. Birch, that this King, as well as Nantef IV., was anterior to the Twelfth Dynasty, and that he was succeeded by a brother named Nantef. This enables us to supply the destroyed nomen, No. 16, between Nantef I. and Nantef III., in the list of the Chamber of Kings, and to decide that the partly-effaced nomen, No. 18, is that of Nantef IV.

The nomen of Nantef III. is the same as that of Nantef I., which I have just given: his prenomen has not been found. We know nothing of the events of his reign, excepting such events as belong to the history of other Dynasties, and that of Egypt generally, which probably fell in that period.

Respecting Nantef IV., we know as little as we do of his predecessor. His prenomen and nomen have been found, and I here insert them. He has a title which I

cannot certainly interpret, in his nomen.

In the reign of the next King, Munt-hotp, we again find direct monumental evidence of the contemporaneousness of two Dynasties. The prenomen of Munt-hotp, which I here insert with his nomen, reads

Neb-tete-ra, that is, "Pharaoh, lord of Upper and Lower Egypt." In a tablet on the Kuseyr Road (a road which crosses the Desert between the Thebaïd and the Red Sea), we find the following royal names: a prenomen, inclosed in a royal ring (which Mr. Burton, in his "Excerpta Hieroglyphica," gives in characters which read "Si-n-hes-ra," but M. Prisse, in his supplement to Champollion's "Monumens de l'Égypte et de la Nubie," gives differently), preceded by the title "Lord of all Egypt;" with the prenomen of Amenemha I., also enclosed in a royal ring; and the name "Munt-hotp;" both preceded by a title which I cannot read, and that of "chief." Dr. Tomlinson, the learned Bishop of Gibraltar, has already directed the attention of students to this tablet. In another tablet, to be more fully noticed hereafter, we find the name "Amenemha," not enclosed in a royal ring, but with the title "King" given by Munt-hotp, whose name is enclosed in a royal ring, and who is thus identified with the chief Munt-hotp; and the same tablet also shows us that Amenemha I. was confirmed in his kingdom by Munt-hotp. Hence we ascertain that Munt-hotp, the fifth King of the Ninth Dynasty, was contemporary with Amenemha I., the last King of the Eleventh Dynasty. Perhaps the prenomen which occurs in the upper part of the first tablet which I have been noticing is that of the second predecessor of Munt-hotp, Nantef III.; for (whether we follow the copy of Mr. Burton or that of M. Prisse) we do not know it to be the prenomen of any predecessor of Amenemha I., nor of any Diospolite King, nor is it the prenomen of the immediate predecessor of Munt-hotp. I formerly held it to be most probably a variation of the prenomen of Papa, of the Sixth Dynasty; but I think that my opinion was not based upon sufficiently satisfactory grounds; especially since I have found that M. Prisse gives it differently.

This is not an unfit place in which to notice a proof of the partial contemporaneousness of the Ninth Dynasty with the Eleventh and Twelfth, and with the Fifteenth, deducible from the names of persons who lived in the time of the Twelfth Dynasty. It was customary among the ancient Egyptians to name some of their children after the reigning King and other Kings of his Dynasty; so that we find the names Sesertesen and Amenemha very prevalent during the time of the Twelfth Dynasty; whereas we find those names seldom applied to persons not born in the time of Kings bearing them: for example, I have found only one Amenemha after the time of the Kings of that name. Now it is very remarkable that Nantef and Snufre, the former the name of five of the first six Kings of the Ninth Dynasty, the latter the prenomen of the second Shepherd-King of the Fifteenth Dynasty, are very commonly applied to individuals who lived in the time of the Twelfth Dynasty; a fact which, if we had no other evidence, would indicate that the Ninth and Fifteenth Dynasties immediately preceded in time, or were partly contemporaneous with, the Twelfth; thus affording another independent argument for the scheme of contemporaneousness which I have adopted. But what is still more remarkable is this; that we find a similar correspondence in the nomens and prenomens of Kings. Nufre-ka-ra and its variations are found as nomens in the Second, and Fifth Dynasties, and, as prenomens in the Eleventh, and Fifteenth Dynasties *. We find two Mencherêses, Men-ka-ra of the Second Dynasty, and Men-kau-ra of the Fourth, nearly, if not quite, contemporaries. In like manner, we find two Papas, one in the Second Dynasty, and the other in the Sixth, in like manner, nearly, if not quite, contemporaries. On the other hand, we find scarcely any instances of Kings at distant intervals bearing the same or similar nomens or prenomens. This inquiry might be carried to a still further length; but I think that I have said enough to satisfy any candid mind that the names of men, as well as of Kings, furnish remarkable arguments for the scheme of contemporaneousness explained in this work.

We know some other particulars of the history of the time of Munt-hotp; but these will be more properly discussed in the examination of that of the Eleventh Dynasty. The Shepherd-invasion, the great event of this part of the ancient Egyptian history, took place in the reign of this King or in that of his predecessor. Of the last of the Heracleopolites men-

* On referring to the table of the hieroglyphic names of the Kings of the first Seventeen Dynasties, it will be seen that part of the Second Dynasty was contemporary with part of the Fifth, and terminated about the time of the commencement of the Fifteenth, being also partly contemporary with the Eleventh Dynasty.

tioned in the list of the Chamber of Kings, the successor of Munt-hotp, whose name is partly erased, but was doubtless Nantef (V.), we know nothing but that in that list he is only called "Chief," and his name appears not to have been enclosed in a ring, though this part of the list is so much erased as to render it uncertain. I have already mentioned the probable reason why Thothmes III. does not treat this personage as a King. The history of the subsequent Kings of this Dynasty, and of all those of the Tenth, is unknown; and I have already given the most probable Chronology of the two Dynasties.

The Diospolite Kingdom commenced with the Eleventh Dynasty, which was partly contemporary with the Sixth and Ninth. Of the Kings of this Dynasty we know very little, and they evidently did not possess much power. Its chronology also presents considerable difficulties. Manetho says that it consisted of sixteen Kings, who reigned forty-three years; after whom Ammenemês reigned sixteen years. Thus it appears that, if we include Ammenemês, (Amenemha I.,) who does not appear to be assigned to this or the succeeding Dynasty, strictly speaking, the sum would be seventeen Kings and fifty-nine years. In the list of the Chamber of ings, we find only eight Kings of this Dynasty, the legitimate Kings; but in the Turin Papyrus we find several others, seven in number. This portion of the latter list is preceded by a prenomen, partly effaced, which is probably that of Amenemha I., whose prenomen twice occurs among the names that follow; so that altogether there are ten names, including the seven first mentioned; and thus the Turin Papyrus gives at least seven Kings more than the List of the Chamber of Kings. This suggests, (as, I believe, Dr. Hincks was the first to remark,) that several of the Kings of the Eleventh Dynasty were usurpers, and that Amenemha I. was probably at least twice deposed, and afterwards restored to the throne. Part of this King's prenomen, or a similar name, occurs before the place of the first King of Manetho's Twelfth Dynasty, in another part of the same list. The monuments shew that Amenemha I. was the co-regent of Sesertesen I., the first King of the Twelfth Dynasty, for part of his reign; and this, added to what Manetho says, indicates his second restoration. The sixteen years' reign of Amenemha I., mentioned by Manetho, probably refers to the time during which that King reigned after the commencement of the Twelfth Dynasty. Since the portion of the Eleventh Dynasty which I have mentioned above, in the Royal Turin Papyrus, is only in a fragment, and since another fragment apparently contains the prenomens Nos. 3 and 5 of the list of the Chamber of Kings, with the omission of No. 4, but both partly erased, it appears that Manetho is right in assigning sixteen Kings to the Dynasty, exclusive of Amenemha I. It is not so easy to form a probable opinion as to the duration of the Dynasty; for forty-three years seems, at first sight, far too short a sum; and that it is really so is proved by our having the date of the forty-sixth year of the King whose prenomen reads Neb-tu-ra[*]. Perhaps it commenced shortly after the Ninth Dynasty. The only remarkable King of this Dynasty was Amenemha I., the Ammen-

[*] Champollion's Deux Lettres au Duc de Blacas, Pl. XV.

emês of Manetho. Perhaps the Shepherd-invasion happened during his reign, though I think it most probable that it took place in that of an earlier King. There is an important tablet relating to this King on the Kuseyr Road, a copy of which is given in Plate V. of Mr. Burton's Excerpta. It commences thus: "The second year, the fifteenth day of Paôphi, [of the reign of] the Horus, lord of Upper and Lower Egypt, lord of Upper Egypt, lord of Lower Egypt, lord of Upper and Lower Egypt, the gold of the gods, King of all Egypt, Neb-tete-ra, the son of the sun, Munt-hotp, living for ever." I have translated all these titles to shew that a King who calls himself lord of all Egypt, &c., was not necessarily sole sovereign, as I have already had occasion to observe. After some more titles, &c., we read, "The lord of all Egypt, Neb-tete-ra, living for ever, like the sun, says, I will establish his majesty, the illustrious, the chief, ... chief of the buildings, the magnanimous, [literally fullhearted] King, Amenemha [L], with soldiers, ... in Upper Egypt." In the fourteenth line of the same tablet, we find a mention of Munt-hotp's having appointed a certain person, called the chief of the "foreigners," over, or chief of, Upper and Lower Egypt. What I have translated "foreigners" is the group which I give in Plate VII. No. 5, and which probably reads "Penu," or Phœnicians. From this record we ascertain that Munt-hotp, at the time supreme King, made Amenemha I. King of Upper Egypt, or confirmed him in his kingdom, endeavouring by an alliance with him to counteract the power of the Shepherds. It appears also that he was forced by the Shepherds, who seem to have flattered him by acknowledging him as supreme King, to give one of their chiefs an important title, which would oblige the Egyptians to acknowledge his authority to a certain extent.

The Fourteenth Dynasty, or Xoite Kingdom, may have commenced during the time of the Eleventh; but as it more probably commenced with, or during the time of, the Twelfth, I shall notice it hereafter.

I have now concluded the examination of that part of the history of Egypt which relates to the period before the Shepherd-invasion, and I have somewhat overpassed my proper limits in treating of the Eleventh Dynasty until its conclusion, which was subsequent to that invasion by a few years. This I have done for the sake of clearness.

SECTION IV.

HISTORY OF THE PERIOD OF THE SHEPHERD-DOMINATION.

IN the present section I shall consider the most remarkable memorials of a period of more than five hundred years, during the greater part of which, chiefly after the time of the Twelfth Dynasty, the Shepherd-Kings appear to have been predominant. This portion of the history of Egypt is the more interesting on account of the manner in which it illustrates that of neighbouring countries at this remote period.

Before considering the account which Manetho gives of the invasion of Egypt by the Shepherds, it will be proper to inquire what causes led to that remarkable event, and how it came to pass that Egypt was so easily subjugated by the foreign invaders.

In the fourteenth chapter of Genesis, we are told that a great confederation of Kings, Amraphel, King of Shinar, Arioch, King of Ellasar, Chedorlaomer, King of Elam, (Persia,) and Tidal, King of the Goim, or Gentiles, invaded Palestine, and compelled the Kings of "the cities of the plain" to become tributaries of Chedorlaomer, the chief of the confederation. "Twelve years they served Chedorlaomer, and in the thirteenth year they rebelled. And in the fourteenth year came Chedorlaomer, and the Kings that [were] with him, and smote the Rephaims in Ashteroth Karnaim, and the Zuzims in Ham, and the Emims in Shaveh Kiriathaim, and the Horites in their Mount Seir, unto El-paran, which [is] by the wilderness. And they returned, and came to En-mishpat, which [is] Kadesh, and smote all the country of the Amalekites, and also the Amorites, that dwell in Hazezon-tamar." Having recorded these events, the sacred historian proceeds to relate the defeat of the Kings of the cities of the plain by the four confederate monarchs, whose names are again given, and whose overthrow by Abraham is afterwards narrated. I have been particular in quoting part of this passage verbatim, to prevent misapprehension of the position of some of the conquered nations. As Khem is the hieroglyphic name of Egypt, as the Shepherd-invasion evidently took place about the time of Chedorlaomer's expeditions, and as a Ham was conquered during those expeditions, it might be supposed that the confederate monarchs conquered Egypt, and that the Shepherds were garrisons left by them; but this would be an erroneous idea: Ham, when applied to Egypt, is written with Heth; (חם;) but here Ham is written with He; (הם;) and even if we allow that, by a mistake of a copyist, Heth may have been changed to He, in consequence of the similarity of the two letters, the order of march shews that this Ham can only have been somewhere in Palestine.

The dates of the two invasions of Palestine which we are considering are not easily fixed with great exactness. All we know is, that the second happened between Abraham's journey to Palestine from Haran and the birth of Ishmael, therefore between the years B.C. 2082 and 2071; and consequently the date of the first would be between the years B.C. 2095 and 2084, according to Hales's chronology, slightly corrected by me. I shall shew that the reign of the first Shepherd-King commenced about this time; and the Shepherd-invasion evidently happened not many years before his reign. It appears to me that the first invasion of Palestine by Chedorlaomer and his confederates probably caused the Shepherds to leave the East, and settle in Egypt. Further, Manetho tells us that Salatis built Avaris from his fear of the Assyrians, who were "then increasing in power," and by whom Manetho probably means the confederate monarchs. Such an event as Chedorlaomer's first expedition must have unsettled many powerful tribes of those countries whence the Shepherds came. It is also probable that the "grievous" famine which compelled Abraham to visit Egypt caused a considerable influx of Shepherd-settlers. The second famine, which caused Isaac to go to Gerar, must have had the same effect.

Manetho tells us that the Shepherds easily gained possession of Egypt without a battle. When we see from the monuments how powerful Egypt was when ruled by the Kings of the Fourth Dynasty and their contemporaries, it naturally surprises us to read such an account of its subjugation. It seems to me, however, that it is not difficult to see the probable cause. For more than six centuries, from the time of Mênês, the founder of the monarchy, to the Shepherd-invasion, it appears that the Egyptians enjoyed a long period of prosperity; and, contented with the natural fertility of their own country, did not seek to enrich themselves by foreign conquest. Indeed they do not appear to have engaged in any external war, further than in occasional expeditions beyond the boundaries to repress the incursions of Nomadic tribes; and, possibly, in inroads into the interior of Africa for slaves, ivory, and other objects of trade. But this long period of prosperity had its usual results: the inhabitants became indolent and luxurious, and the kingdom became separated into small states. When this state of things had long continued, and a peace of great duration had produced, as we may conclude, delusive feelings of security, the Shepherds invaded Egypt. This, however, would explain the circumstance that the Shepherds conquered Egypt, but not that they conquered it without a battle. How could this have been the case, when that country was populous, and its inhabitants were not unacquainted with the art of war? I think it probable that some one of the Egyptian Kings, to recover his rightful supremacy, or to destroy the power of a dangerous rival, adopted the unwise expedient of inviting foreigners to aid him in attaining his object. The sudden appearance of a large force of foreigners, in alliance with an Egyptian King, would have awed the other Kings, his contemporaries, and induced them to become tributaries, rather than to risk everything upon an unequal contest. Then the Shepherds would not hesitate to consider their own interests, and forget those of him who had invited them. The history of the world, in all ages, affords instances of the same kind; but my explanation of this event is, of course, based upon probabilities and conjecture; though I think that it is the only one that can be offered, and it is not inconsistent with the last inscription which I have noticed.

Manetho gives us a most circumstantial and interesting account of the invasion and conquest of Egypt by the Shepherds, which is preserved by Josephus in his tract against Apion. From its great importance, it will not be amiss to give this narrative in full, with a commentary on the most remarkable statements which it contains.

The historian begins by saying, " We had [formerly]

a King whose name was Timaios (or Timaos)." This King's name does not occur in Manetho's lists; and from the time at which the Shepherd-invasion took place, we can only say that he must have belonged to the Second, Fifth, Sixth, Ninth, Eleventh, or Fourteenth, Dynasty.

" In his time, [it came to pass,] I know not how, that God was displeased, and [there came], in a strange manner, from the East, men of an ignoble race, [who] had the confidence to invade the country, and easily subdued it by their power without a battle."

The Egyptians called these invaders " Shepherds," and " Hycsôs," or " Shepherd-kings," according to Manetho's statements. Respecting their race, he (or Josephus, perhaps,) says, in a subsequent place to that which I am now considering, that some said they were Arabs. In the list of the Dynasties, the Kings of the First Dynasty of Shepherds, those who reigned at Memphis, are called Phœnicians. This seems to be confirmed by what Herodotus says respecting the temenos, or sacred grove, of Proteus, at Memphis. He remarks, " Phœnicians of Tyre dwell round this temenos, and this whole tract is called the Camp of the Tyrians." (περιοικέουσι δὲ τὸ τέμενος τοῦτο Φοίνικες Τύριοι· καλέεται δὲ ὁ χῶρος οὗτος ὁ συνάπας Τυρίων στρατόπεδον.) The historian adds, that "in the temenos of Proteus is a temple, which is called that of the foreign Aphrodite."* The name of the Camp of the Tyrians seems to me to point to the time of the taking of Memphis by the first Shepherds, some of the descendants, or reputed descendants, of whom may have continued to live at Memphis in the time of Herodotus.

* Herod. ii. 112.

THE SHEPHERDS.

The foreign Aphrodite can scarcely be doubted to be Ashtaroth, called by the Greeks "Astarte," whose name is found at the quarries of Tura, opposite Memphis, in a tablet of the time of Amenoph II. We shall see, however, in a future place, that there is abundant evidence to show that the Shepherds did not consist of but one race, although their first Kings may have been Phœnicians of Tyre. It is evident that many foreign settlers of different races came to Egypt during the Shepherd-period, and it is not improbable that the first Shepherds who invaded that country were of several tribes. In the monumental inscriptions we find mention of "Shepherds,"[*] "Phœnicians?"[†] and "Enemies;"[‡] and in the inscriptions of the time of Sethee I., the first King of Manetho's Nineteenth Dynasty, "Enemies of the land of Shasu."[§] I shall show, in a subsequent place, that the "Enemies of the land of Shasu" appear to have been of the same race as some or all of the first Shepherds, and to have invaded Egypt a second time, and been expelled by Sethee I., in the first year of his reign. Manetho continues his narrative in the following words:

"And having subdued the rulers, they also burnt up the cities, and demolished the temples of the gods; and they acted most cruelly to all the natives, slaying some, and making slaves of the children and wives of others."

The manner in which the Shepherds pillaged Egypt and maltreated its inhabitants may perhaps have been

---

[*] See Plate VII., No. 6.
[†] See Plate VII., No. 5.
[‡] See Plate VII., No. 7, latter half.
[§] See Plate VII., No. 12, first twelve characters.

somewhat exaggerated by some of Manetho's authorities, from the bitter hatred which the Egyptians had for those foreign tribes at a later period; but there is evidence of the ruin which they effected among the monuments of Egypt. No temples remain of the time before the Shepherd-invasion, and few monuments of the time of the Shepherd-rule. Their destruction is not, however, to be wholly attributed to the foreign subjugators. We must not forget that it is generally acknowledged, from what remains of them, that the temples constructed before the time of the Eighteenth Dynasty were in most cases smaller, and less strong in construction, than those of later times. I shall be able to show that Manetho misrepresents the Kings of the Fifteenth Dynasty; some of whom, at least, instead of being tyrants and oppressors, were benefactors to the Egyptian race: but perhaps this is the fault of Manetho's authorities. The invasion and subjugation of Egypt by the Shepherds must have been the chief cause of the remarkable changes which then took place in the Dynasties which ruled that country. The Memphite kingdom was for a time supplanted by that of the Shepherds of the Fifteenth Dynasty, who seized the city founded by Mênês, and continued to reign there for little less than three centuries. The Eleventh Dynasty, after a time of confusion, was succeeded by the Twelfth, which soon appears to have deprived the Heracleopolites and Elephantinites of much of their power; though the Fifth Dynasty, and most probably the Ninth, continued for a long time afterwards. About this time also, it appears that the Second Dynasty, the later Kings of which seem to have had but little power, came to an end. The Xoite Kingdom commenced about the same time; but we have no evidence to show that its Kings extended their rule beyond the northern parts of Lower Egypt. The whole of Egypt was virtually divided between the Diospolites of the Twelfth Dynasty, who ruled Upper Egypt, and the Shepherds of the Fifteenth, who ruled Lower Egypt. Middle Egypt was probably for the most part under the dominion of the Diospolites. This state of things continued for more than a century and a half.

I shall now consider the chronology and history of the Twelfth Dynasty. It has been shown from the monuments, that certain of the Kings of this Dynasty reigned conjointly with others; Amenemha II. beginning to reign in the reign of Sesertesen L; and Seserteseu II., in that of Amenemha II.; and Sesertesen I. and Amenemha I., as well as probably Amenemha III. and the King whose prenomen reads Ma-tu-ra, being for a time, at least, colleagues. All these Kings, excepting Amenemha I., belong to the Twelfth Dynasty. The uncertainty as to whether Sesertesen III. and Ra-sebak-nufre reigned conjointly with other sovereigns, and as to the length of the reigns of particular Kings, makes it impossible to fix the chronology of this Dynasty with exactness. I now give two tables: the second being a list of the Twelfth Dynasty partly conjectural; and the first, the lists upon which it is chiefly based. I mark the conjectural parts of these tables with notes of interrogation.

TABLES OF THE TWELFTH DYNASTY.

I.

Manetho, according to Africanus.		Turin Papyrus.				Mon. name.	Most probable length of reign.
	Years.		Years.	Ms.	Ds.		Years. Ms.
1. Sesonchôsis	. . 46	 45		x	x	Sesertesen (L)	. 45
2. Ammanemês	. . 38	 xx		x	x	Amenemha (II.)	. 38
		 19		x	x	Sesertesen (II.)	. 19
3. Sesôstris	. . . 48	. . . . . 3x		x	x	Sesertesen (III.)	. 38?
4. Lacharês	. . . 8	. . . . . 4x		x	x	Amenemha III.	. 42?
5. Amerês	. . . 8						
		(In another Fragment.)					
6. Amenemês	. . 8	Ma-tu-ra	. 9	3	27	Ma-tu-ra . . .	9 3
7. Skemiophris	. . 4	Ra-sebak-nufre 3		10	24	Ra-sebak-nufre .	3 10
		(Sum)	. 213*	1	1x	Sum about	195 1

* This sum probably includes the reign of the King next before Sesertesen I., in the Papyrus, who is probably Amenemha I.: its length is x9.

II.

				Remarkable events in Kings' reigns.
Sesertesen I.		Amenemha I.		
	. . 43	Amenemha II.	. . 1	B.C. 2005. First Tropical Cycle.
Sesertesen II.	. . 1		33	
	. .	Sesertesen III.		B.C. 1986. Phœnix of Sesostris.
Amenemha III.	. . 1			
	. . 30?	Ma-tu-ra	1?	
	. . 39?	Ra-sebak-nufre . .	1?	

The correspondences of the years of Sesertesen I. and Amenemha IL, and of Amenemha II. and Sesertesen IL, are on the authority of the monuments. The co-regency of Sesertesen II. with Sesertesen III., and of Amenemha III. with Ra-sebak-nufre and Ma-tu-ra, I only consider probable. With respect to the latter case, my conjecture is founded upon Eusebius's having said that the later Kings of this Dynasty reigned forty-two years. It is most probable that the Twelfth and Fifteenth Dynasties commenced about the same time.

I have already mentioned that Munt-hotp, of the Ninth Dynasty, Amenemha I., of the Eleventh, and a chief of the Shepherds, were contemporary. From this it might be supposed that the first King of the Fifteenth Dynasty began to reign before the commencement of the Twelfth Dynasty; but, in the first place, it must be remembered that Amenemha I. was, for part of his reign, a co-regent of Sesertesen I., the first King of the latter Dynasty; and, in the second place, that the Shepherd-chief mentioned above may not have been a Shepherd-king. I can now notice the history of Manetho's Twelfth Dynasty.

Sesertesen I., the first King of the Twelfth Dy-

nasty, was one of the most powerful sovereigns of the period that preceded the Eighteenth Dynasty, and there are many records still preserved among the monuments of Egypt which show the extent of his power. The two most famous of the Sesertesens were the First and Third; the former of whom may be called Sesôstris the conqueror; the latter, Sesôstris the lawgiver: the latter is Manetho's Sesôstris, and was worshipped by some later Kings, being esteemed far before the conqueror, though he may also have signalized himself by military exploits. Two obelisks, that of Heliopolis, near Cairo, and that of Bigeeg, in the province called the Feiyoom, are of the time of Sesertesen I. They possess great interest, not only from their antiquity, being about coëval, in my opinion, with the time of the patriarch Abraham, but also from their being the oldest monuments of their kind known to remain.

There is another remarkable record of this King's reign, a list of conquered or tributary tribes or countries, the most ancient yet discovered, on a tablet found by Dr. Ricci at Wádee Halfeh, in Nubia, near the Second Cataracts. Rosellini gives a copy of it*; and Champollion first described it†. It has not been satisfactorily ascertained to what tribes or countries these names apply. I have already mentioned that Amenemha I. was a colleague of Sesertesen I. for some time. This was doubtless early in the reign of the latter King.

In the forty-third year of Sesertesen I., his second colleague, Amenemha II., began to reign, and reigned,

according to Manetho, thirty-eight years. There is a small temple of the time of Amenemha II. and Sesertesen II. at Wádee Gásoos, near the Egyptian shore of the Red Sea. (Wilkinson's "Modern Egypt and Thebes," ii. 385.) In the reign of Amenemha II., the first Tropical Cycle commenced, on January the 7th, B.C. 2005. This is the second date which I have found recorded on the Egyptian monuments: the first so recorded being the commencement of the second Great Panegyrical Year, B.C. 2352, in the time of the two Sûphises.

* Monumenti Storici, Pl. XXV., No. 4.
† Lettres, p. 124.

CHRONOLOGICAL REMARKS.

I must here deviate from my present subject, to show how the interval between the Sûphises and Amenemha II., according to Manetho's lists, as they have come down to us, corrected by means of the monuments, may be compared with the system of chronology which I have put forth. The successors of the Sûphises are stated by Africanus to have reigned 126 years: the Fourth Dynasty was immediately succeeded by the Sixth, which lasted, according to Africanus, corrected for reasons already stated, 143 years: at the conclusion of the latter Dynasty, unless the seventy days' reign of the Seventh Dynasty intervened, the Fifteenth Dynasty commenced; and about the same time, the Twelfth; and Amenemha II. began to reign in the forty-third year of Sesertesen I., the first King of the Twelfth Dynasty. Thus the whole interval from the accession of Mencherês to that of Amenemha II. is about 311 years, according to the best version of Manetho, with certain corrections; and the interval from the beginning of the second Great Panegyrical Year, in the time of the two Sûphises, to that of the first Tropical Cycle is 347 years. This shows that my dates agree in a remarkable manner with Manetho corrected by the monuments. There is also another argument which would lead us to the same results with reference to the interval from the Fourth to the Twelfth Dynasty. The sculptures of the time of the Fourth Dynasty bear such a near resemblance to those of the time of the Twelfth, that when we find a sculpture of either of these two periods, it is almost impossible to say to which period it belongs until we see in it a royal name. The difference between the sculptures and hieroglyphics of the Twelfth Dynasty and those of the commencement of the Eighteenth Dynasty, separated by a period of four or five hundred years, is very strongly marked. During the Eighteenth Dynasty, as well as the Nineteenth and Twentieth, we can often distinguish the sculptures of the time of one King from those of the time of another a century later, by the style. When the arts in Egypt had attained their highest degree of excellence, their decline commenced, and continued until the time of the Twenty-sixth Dynasty, when there was a remarkable revival; but the decline of the arts continued after this uninterruptedly until the time of the latest monuments: and throughout this long period, we can generally distinguish the relative ages of monuments by the style of their sculptures and paintings when separated by an interval equal to that which I find to have divided the Sûphises from the Twelfth Dynasty. Thus the chronology of the Egyptian monuments, confirmed by the style of their sculptures and inscriptions, shows the length of the interval from the Sûphises to Amenemha II.; while Manetho, according to Africanus, properly understood, agrees as to the duration of the period in question. This, it should be remarked, is the most disputed part of Egyptian Chronology; there being but little dispute concerning the interval from Mênês to the Sûphises. I must beg the reader to remember, in this place, the authorities upon which the ascertaining of the length of the interval from the Sûphises to Amenemha II. is based. They are inscriptions on the Egyptian monuments, copied by me, so that I have not to rely upon others, and can myself put them forth with confidence: and the calculations by which these inscriptions have been elucidated, originally made by me, have been again made at the Royal Observatory, and the calculations there made have been verified by Mr. Airy himself, the Astronomer Royal.

Sesertesen II. became the colleague of Amenemha

II. in the thirty-third year of the reign of the latter King. Sesertesen III., Manetho's Sesôstris, who was

afterwards worshipped, apparently as a great lawgiver, was probably for some time a co-regent of Sesertesen II., succeeding Amenemha II. In the reign of Sesertesen III., occurs that most important date, the commencement of the Third Great Panegyrical Year, and the First Phœnix Cycle, called the appearance of the Phœnix of Sesôstris, in the year B.C. 1986. I have already had occasion, in the first Part of this work, to give my reasons for concluding that Sesertesen III. was Manetho's Sesôstris. In the lists we find a short account of the conquests of Sesôstris, which can scarcely be doubted to be more applicable to Sesertesen I. than to Sesertesen III., and still more so to Rameses II.

The successor of Sesôstris is called, in the lists, "Lacharês," "Lamaris," or "Lampares"; and we are told that he built the Labyrinth in the Arsinoïte nome, as a tomb for himself. The successor of Manetho's Sesôstris in the Tablet of Abydos is Amenemha III.,

whose prenomen reads " Ma-en-ra." He may be the Mœris of the Greeks.

Among the hieroglyphic inscriptions of Wádee Maghárah, we find one (a copy of which was given by Lord Prudhoe, now the Duke of Northumberland, and Colonel Felix, to Mr. Burton, for his " Excerpta Hieroglyphica "), which throws much light upon the history of this period. This tablet* is divided into three compartments. The first of these is dated in the third year of Amenemha III., and does not seem to contain any important information. The second compartment commences with the date of the forty-first year of the same King, and gives the following name (which reads

Seser-hotp-ret) and the titles of a King, who is probably of the Ninth Dynasty, but, perhaps, of the Fourteenth. The third compartment contains the name and titles of a foreign King, Snufre, whose name

* Excerpta Hieroglyphica, Pl. XII.

THE SHEPHERD-DYNASTIES. 163

is differently written from the synonymous prenomen of Bêôn. This part is dated in the forty-second year of the reign of Amenemha III., about which time it is probable that the Twelfth Dynasty concluded. Snufre is called the ruler of several foreign lands. I cannot doubt that this Snufre was a King of the Sixteenth Dynasty. This important tablet, therefore, plainly points out the contemporaneousness, in part, of three Dynasties, the Twelfth, the Sixteenth, and another Dynasty, which is either the Ninth or the Fourteenth.

I have already mentioned my opinion that the King whose prenomen reads " Ma-tu-ra"[1] and Ra-sebak-nufre[2]

were probably co-regents of Amenemha III. I now return to the consideration of the history of the Shepherds in Egypt.

The whole duration of the Shepherd-Dynasties cannot easily be determined, and the variations between Africanus and Eusebius and Josephus make it impossible to decide what Manetho wrote on this subject. This will appear from the following table, which contains what Africanus and Eusebius and Josephus say respecting the length of the Fifteenth, Sixteenth, and

M 2

Seventeenth Dynasties, and the number of Kings of which they consisted. I have made two transpositions in this table; putting the Seventeenth Dynasty in Eusebius's list opposite the Fifteenth in Africanus's; and the Fifteenth in the former list opposite the Seventeenth in the latter. This I have done because the Fifteenth Dynasty in Africanus's list evidently corresponds to the Seventeenth in Eusebius's.

TABLE OF THE SHEPHERD-DYNASTIES.

AFRICANUS.	EUSEBIUS.	JOSEPHUS.
Fifteenth Dynasty.	*Seventeenth Dynasty.*	
Six Shepherd-Kings who reigned 284 years.	Four Shepherd-Kings who reigned 103 years.	Six Shepherd-Kings who reigned 259 years, 10 months.
Sixteenth Dynasty.	*Sixteenth Dynasty.*	
Thirty-two Shepherd-Kings who reigned 518 years.	Five Theban Kings who reigned 190 years.	
Seventeenth Dynasty.	*Fifteenth Dynasty.*	
Forty-three Theban Kings and forty-three Shepherd-Kings who reigned 151 years.	Diospolite Kings who reigned 250 years.	

Before noticing the difficulties occasioned by the extraordinary disagreements between the copyists, I shall make some remarks on the chronology of the period.

The date of the commencement of the First Tropical Cycle, in the time of Amenemha II., shows that the Twelfth Dynasty commenced in one of the years B.C. 2084 to 2047, inclusive; and the Fifteenth Dynasty must have commenced about the same time. Josephus tells us, from Manetho, that the Shepherds ruled over Egypt for five hundred and eleven years, until the Kings of the Thebaïd and of the rest of

Egypt made an insurrection against them. The date of the commencement of the Eighteenth Dynasty, which is the latest date that we can assign to the revolt against the Shepherds, is about the year B.C. 1525; and therefore, if Manetho's five hundred and eleven years be correct, the latest date we can assign to the commencement of the Fifteenth Dynasty will be about the year B.C. 2036; and it seems to me most probable that it commenced about half a century earlier.

Josephus and Africanus agree in assigning to the Fifteenth Dynasty six Kings, though the former makes its duration twenty-five years less than the latter. The difference lies in the length of the reign of the third King, Apachnas, which is stated to have been thirty-six years by Josephus, but sixty-one by Africanus. We cannot decide which is the more accurate of the two copyists in this instance. There is also another difference between these two writers; for Josephus places Apôphis, whom Africanus makes the last King of the Dynasty, between Apachnas and Iannas, making him the fourth King of the Dynasty. In the list of the Chamber of Kings, a prenomen, which is shown by the Royal Turin Papyrus to be that of Apachnas, immediately precedes the nomen of Iannas; and therefore it is most probable that Josephus is wrong in placing Apôphis between these two Kings. I say most probable, since sometimes Kings mentioned by Manetho are omitted in the monumental lists, although they have left monuments, because they were not considered legitimate sovereigns by those who made these lists.

The monuments do not enable us to decide as to the correctness or incorrectness of the statement of Africanus respecting the number of Kings, or the duration, of the Sixteenth Dynasty. He is, however, manifestly wrong as to the number of the Kings of the Seventeenth Dynasty. I have no doubt that this Dynasty was one of Shepherd-Kings only, and not of Thebans also; since it is evident that the Thirteenth Dynasty ruled from the conclusion of the Twelfth to the commencement of the Eighteenth. It appears to me most probable that the Sixteenth Dynasty was partly contemporary with the Fifteenth, and that it lasted long after it; and that the Seventeenth ruled during the later part of the period from the conclusion of the Twelfth Dynasty to the commencement of the Eighteenth.

To return to what Manetho says respecting the Shepherds in Egypt. After speaking of the cruelties which the Shepherds inflicted upon the conquered people, he continues his narration in the following words: "And at length they made one of themselves King, whose name was Salatis. He lived at Memphis, making the Upper and Lower Country to pay tribute, and placing garrisons in the most fit situations."

From this it is evident that some time elapsed after the invasion of Egypt by the Shepherds before they made for themselves a King, according to Manetho; but we have no reason to suppose that the period was one of many years. The prenomen of Salatis is found on the monuments, and it is also given in the Royal Turin Papyrus, where it is written without the sign Ra. It reads, in the former case, "Nufre-ka-ra."

It is important here to notice a proof of the contemporaneousness of certain of the first seventeen Dynasties with others of that portion of Manetho's list, which would be sufficient to establish, on monumental evidence, the contemporaneousness of the Memphites, Heracleopolites, Diospolites, Xoites, and Shepherds. On account of the great importance of this fact, I give one of the lists of Chenoboscion (from my own copy), a portion of the list of the Chamber of Kings, and a fragment of the Royal Turin Papyrus, in Plate VII, Nos. 1, 2, 3, and 4. The reader will see that the arrangement is as follows :—

DYN.	ROYAL TURIN PAPYRUS.	LIST OF CHENOBOSCION.	LIST OF CHAMBER OF KINGS.
VI.		Papa.	[Pa]pa.
,,		Mer-en-ra.	Mer-en-ra.
,,	Net-akartee.		
XV.	Nufre-ka.	Nufre-ka-ra.	. . . .
,,	Snufre.		Snufre.
,,	Ab		Shura.

All the names in this table, excepting Papa, Netakartee, and Ab . . . ., are prenomens. The numbers of the Dynasties are from Manetho.

With respect to the fragment of the Royal Turin Papyrus, it is necessary to remark, that it is but one fragment, not two joined together. Each of the three lists of Chenoboscion contains three names in the same order, with no difference but that one gives the prenomen (Mee-ra) instead of the nomen (Papa) of Phiôps, and that the first two characters of the same King's name in one list are indistinct. Sir Gardner Wilkinson first discovered these lists, as I have before mentioned, and published a copy of one of them in his "Ancient Egyptians." * Two of the lists are in hori-

* Vol. iii., p. 280.

zontal lines, and the third is in perpendicular : a single line containing a King's name and titles in each list. Now from these three records, that is, from the triple monumental record in the grottoes of Chenoboscion, which is of the time of Salatis, and from the Chamber of Kings, also a monumental record, and a national one, of the time of Thothmes III., sculptured in the great temple of Thebes, the metropolis of that time, and from the Royal Turin Papyrus, which, though much injured, is most valuable as the fullest list which has been preserved among the papyri, and in hieratic characters,—from these three remarkable records, we learn that the Fifteenth Dynasty succeeded the Sixth [*]. From this fact, it is obvious that the intermediate kingdoms in Manetho's list, and the kingdoms to which the Sixth and Fifteenth Dynasties belong, were contemporary; and therefore the Memphites were contemporary with the Heracleopolites, Diospolites, Xoites, and Shepherds ; and thus five of the seven columns of the table of contemporary Dynasties are proved : analogy would suffice for proof of the rest; but it is worthy of remark, that the Elephantinite Dynasty contained in one of these two other columns is proved by the monuments to have been partly contemporary with the Fourth and partly with the Fifteenth; and the Kings of the remaining column, the Thinites, are likewise proved to have been contemporary by the Era of the commencement of the Egyptian kingdom, independently of several arguments, derived from the monuments, which would

[*] Perhaps the seventy days' reign of the seventy Kings called the Seventh Dynasty intervened between the Sixth and Fifteenth Dynasties, though it more probably intervened between the Fifteenth and Eighth ; so that it must always be understood, when I speak of the Fifteenth Dynasty as having succeeded the Sixth, that the Seventh Dynasty may have intervened between them.

render this most probable were it not so proved. The contemporaneousness of certain of the first seventeen Dynasties is most satisfactorily proved: the records which I have just adduced would be sufficient to prove this fact even if there were no other indication of it upon the Egyptian monuments; but those monuments, of many ages, during the first seventeen Dynasties, are full of abundant evidence of this great fact of ancient Egyptian history, from the time of the Fourth Dynasty to that of the Fifteenth; that is, from the period of the earliest monuments to the middle of the Shepherd-period. I have dwelt upon this subject at some length because of its very great importance; as, without a knowledge of the contemporaneousness of certain of the first seventeen Dynasties with others of the same portion of Manetho's list, it is impossible to form anything approaching to a correct idea of the chronology of these Dynasties, and to explain either Manetho or the monuments.

To return to what we are told of the Shepherd-Kings. Eusebius and Africanus call the first King of the Fifteenth Dynasty " Saïtês "; and state that from him the Saïte nome received its name. If the latter part of this statement be Manetho's, and not his copyists', it seems that this King's name must have been Saïtês, or something similar, and not Salatis.— From the words of Manetho, cited in page 166, it appears that Salatis rendered the Egyptian Kings tributary to him. We cannot doubt, however, that the Kings of the Twelfth Dynasty were, for many years, at least, independent of the Shepherds.—Manetho continues:

"But he chiefly fortified the eastern provinces, foreseeing that the Assyrians, then increasing in power, would have a desire to invade his kingdom."

I have already shewn the important synchronism probably deducible from this statement of Manetho. It also implies that the Assyrians had a desire to invade Egypt at a later time. Perhaps this refers to Chedorlaomer and his confederates, who may have had such a desire, or perhaps it points to a much later period. We know that in the times of the Ethiopians and Saïtes of the Twenty-fifth and Twenty-sixth Dynasties, the Assyrian and Babylonian Kings waged an almost uninterrupted warfare with their powerful rivals of Egypt, often advancing towards the frontiers of that country; and once, under Nebuchadnezzar, conquering it. We have no authentic accounts of war between the Assyrians or Babylonians and the Egyptians in earlier times. Diodorus Siculus relates that Ninus subdued Egypt and Phœnicia, and that Semiramis passed through all Egypt.

Manetho next says, "And finding, in the Saïte nome, a most suitable city, lying to the east of the Bubastite branch of the Nile, called from some ancient theological reference ($\grave{\alpha}\pi\grave{o}$ $\tau\iota\nu\grave{o}s$ $\grave{\alpha}\rho\chi\alpha\acute{\iota}\alpha s$ $\theta\epsilon o\lambda o\gamma\acute{\iota}\alpha s$,) Avaris, he [Salatis] rebuilt it, and made it very strong with walls, placing in it a multitude of soldiers as a garrison, to the number of two hundred and forty thousand men."

In the preceding passage, we should read "Sethroïte" for "Saïte," with Syncellus. Manetho, also, according to Africanus, (Dyn. 15,) and Eusebius, (Dyn. 17,) in his list of the Dynasties, calls the great city which the Shepherds built "a city in the Sethroïte nome." The position assigned to Avaris with reference to the Nile and the boundary, in the account of the reign of Salatis, just cited, shews the accuracy of the correction. Some clue to the signification of the name of Avaris is obtainable from the fact of Manetho's saying that it was so called from some ancient theological reference, and from his saying in another place that it was a Typhonian city. It is not difficult to ascertain the position of Avaris approximatively from Manetho's statement. The Bubastite branch of the Nile is that commonly called the Pelusiac. In the time of the Romans the Sethroïte nome was the most eastern of all the nomes of Egypt, situated between the Pelusiac branch and the desert, having the Mediterranean Sea to the north, and the Arabian nome to the south. In more ancient times, the nomes were fewer, and consequently, in some cases at least, of greater extent. After relating the building and garrisoning of Avaris, the historian continues thus:

"Hither he came in harvest-time, (or summer, κατὰ θέρειαν,) giving [his troops] allowances of corn and pay, and exercising them diligently in the use of arms, to terrify foreigners. And having reigned nineteen years, he died."

I have now quoted all that Manetho, as cited by Josephus, tells us respecting Salatis. In the list of the Dynasties given by Africanus and Eusebius there is a notice of the Shepherd-invasion which somewhat differs from the account which I have already examined. In the text of Africanus, we read, "The Fifteenth Dynasty: of the Shepherds. They were six foreign Phœnician Kings, who also took Memphis. They also built a city in the Sethroïte nome, whence making an incursion, they subdued the Egyptians."*

* There is a misplacement in a transcript of Africanus, and in the Greek version and Armenian translation of Eusebius; the words "The first of whom," &c., instead of following what I have translated above, being placed between the sentence which there ends

In this statement the invasion of Egypt is erroneously placed by the copyists or epitomizers of Manetho after the building of Avaris.

In about the year B.C. 2081, the patriarch Abraham visited Egypt, before the second invasion of Palestine by Chedorlaomer and his confederates. Perhaps Salatis was the Pharaoh to whom he came. The King's being called Pharaoh should not lead us to suppose that he was not a Shepherd; for on the monuments of their subjects the Shepherd-Kings of the Fifteenth Dynasty receive the usual titles of Egyptian Kings, and the title Ra, or Phra, that is, Pharaoh, commences the prenomen of Salatis, as well as the prenomens of almost all the other Kings of Manetho's Dynasties.

The second Shepherd-King, called by Africanus and Eusebius "Bnôn," and by Josephus "Bêôn," is called on the monuments Ra-snufre Pi-ankhee. His preno-

men is usually written without the solar disk, thus forming an exception to the general usage. Another instance of a prenomen without the solar disk, or the

with "Memphis," and that commencing "They also," thus, "The Seventeenth Dynasty, Shepherds. They were foreign Phœnician Kings, brothers, who also took Memphis. The first of whom, Saïtês, reigned nineteen years, from whom the Saïte nome was called. They also built a city in the Sethroïte nome, whence making an incursion, they subdued the Egyptians." (Eus. Gr.) It is worthy of remark, that the Scholiast on the Timæus gives the correct order, although he otherwise agrees with Eusebius in what he says respecting the Shepherd-Kings. (V. Rosellini's Monumenti Storici. T. i. p, 45, note 4.)

figure of the god Ra, is that of Amen-si Pi-hor, the supposed Bocchôris, of the Twenty-fourth Dynasty. The prenomen of Bêôn is found in tombs adjacent to the Pyramids of Memphis. There is a tablet in the British Museum which shews the contemporaneousness of the Twelfth and Fifteenth Dynasties, and that they commenced about the same time. This tablet, a copy of which is given in Plate XIX. of Sharpe's Inscriptions, contains the names of many worshippers, male and female, among whom we find four Snufres. The first eight lines wholly consist of names. In the ninth line, and part of the tenth, we find the usual list of offerings. From near the end of the tenth line to the conclusion of the inscription, we read, " Snufre the son of Setafu, deceased female: he says, I have come to the palace of . . . . the lord of all Egypt, Nub-kau-ra [Amenemha II.,] ever-living." Beneath this are several figures with their names. First, Snufre, son of Setafu, who is represented as a chief, holding in one hand a staff, and in the other, a mace. Before the chief are his brother, sister, and wife; and, lastly, his father, who is called " The ruler, the devotee, his father, Snufre, Ankhee." Here, then, we find a person bearing the nomen and prenomen of Bêôn; for "Ankhee" is equivalent to "Pi-ankhee," "pi" being merely the masculine article, which is more commonly understood than expressed in hieroglyphics. I have shewn how general was the practice of persons taking the sovereign's nomen: we also occasionally find them taking his prenomen, with some title; but here we find a man bearing the nomen and prenomen of a King, not inclosed in royal rings. It is necessary here to remark, that it was not unusual among the ancient Egyptians to bear two names. From this tablet, therefore, we can only conclude that Snufre Ankhee is either Bêôn himself, or a person born in his reign. If the former be the case, it is easily explained by the suggestion that the tablet was sculptured at Abydos or some other place in the Theban Kingdom. In either case, the tablet plainly shews that the Fifteenth Dynasty commenced about the same time as the Twelfth.

The third King of the Fifteenth Dynasty, Apachnas, reigned sixty-one years, according to Africanus's transcript of Manetho's lists. In the list of the Chamber of Kings, we find his prenomen, "Shura;" and in the Royal Turin Papyrus, his nomen, "Ab . . . ." In

the long inscription at Benee-Hasan, a portion of which I have before quoted, (pp. 18, 19,) we find, in the 138th and 139th lines*, a mention of a person called "The chief of the Fields which are of the foreigners." This is a most important corroboration of the evidence which I have adduced to shew that the Shepherds were already in Egypt in the time of Sesertesen II. It appears to me, that what is here called "the Fields," is that part of Lower Egypt called by the Greeks Ἐλεαρχία, τὰ Ἕλη, and Βουκολία; and by the Copts, ⲚⲓⲘⲈϢϢⲰⲦ, "the Fields," or "Plains."

The nomen of Iannas, (according to Josephus,) or

* Burton's Excerpta, Pl. XXXIV.

Staan, (according to Africanus,) the fourth King of the Fifteenth Dynasty, is found on the monuments, and reads "A-an." The name is sometimes somewhat dif-

ferently written; the fish being put as the first, and the reed as the last, character. This King is stated to have reigned fifty years. His prenomen has not yet been identified. His nomen is found, with that of his successor, in a tomb near the Pyramids of El-Geezeh. I shall have to mention some curious particulars connected with this King in treating of the reign of his successor.

Assa, whom Josephus calls Assis, but Africanus and Eusebius, Archlês, succeeded A-an. His prenomen and nomen, which read "Tet-ka-ra Assa," are found

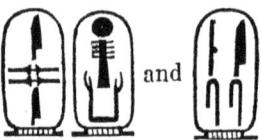

in the tombs of his time in the Necropolis of Memphis. A variation of his nomen is given in the List of the Chamber of Kings. Since the characters composing these nomens are simply alphabetic, it is plain that both are variations of the same name: the only real difference is, that in the latter the final vowel is omitted, and an expletive is introduced. This King is stated to have reigned forty-nine years.

176   THE CITY OF THE LION.   [Part II.

One of the most interesting of the records of the time of Assa is a tomb at Memphis, near the Great Pyramid, which I visited and examined. Among its inscriptions I found some short ones of great importance. The first of these reads, " Assa, the good chief of the city (or land) of the Lion,"* being the nomen of Assa, and one of his titles. The city or land of the Lion must be Leontopolis, or the Leontopolite nome. Among the famous bas-reliefs of Sethee I., (Sethôs,) the first King of Manetho's Nineteenth Dynasty, on the north wall of the great temple of Amen-ra at Thebes, there is one which represents the march of that King, on his return from conquest, into Egypt; and among the cities which he passes, is one which is called " the City of the Lion,"† represented as situated to the east of a branch of the Nile ‡, which is crossed by a bridge, the passage whereof is guarded by a tower or fortress, the name of which is, unfortunately, partially erased §. Another inscription, in another part of the same series of bas-reliefs, dated, like that above mentioned, in the first year of Sethôs, records the overthrow, by that monarch, of "enemies of the land of Shasu . . . . in the fort of the land of the Lion which is towards Kanana (or Canaan);"‖ and afterwards mention is made of " A-ant, their land;"¶ which seems to shew that the people here mentioned were Shepherds, who again invaded Egypt at a late period, and were expelled by Sethôs; for A-ant is evidently in Egypt, from its being mentioned in one of the inscriptions of Munthotp ("Excerpta Hieroglyphica," Pl. III.). I have been

---

* See Plate VII., No. 8.   † See Plate VII., No. 9.
‡ See Plate VII., No. 10.   § See Plate VII., No. 11.
‖ See Plate VII., No. 12.   ¶ See Plate VII., No. 13.

particular in noticing these inscriptions on account of their importance in elucidating the Shepherd history at a period long subsequent to that which I am now considering, and I have noticed them in the present place because they shew satisfactorily that the City or Abode of the Lion was Leontopolis, and the Land of the Lion the Leontopolite Nome. The fortress of the Land of the Lion was evidently in the same nome. I formerly supposed the City of the Lion to be either Leontopolis or Thmuis; and more probably the latter; but from the connexion between the City and Land of the Lion in the inscriptions of Sethee I., I feel convinced of their being, respectively, Leontopolis and the Leontopolite Nome; and my conviction is strengthened by our finding the city mentioned in a manner which shews it to have been a city near the frontier. Thus it appears that Assa, the fifth of the Shepherd-Kings of the Fifteenth Dynasty, ruled not only Memphis, but also, Leontopolis, or the Leontopolite Nome, in the eastern part of the ancient Delta. Another, and similar, short inscription, in the same tomb, reads thus: "Ana, ruler of the city (or land) of Ma . . . ." The royal name in this inscription is a variation of that of Iannas, the predecessor of Assa.

There are other inscriptions of this kind in the same tomb, one of which is important, as containing the title "Establisher of the city of Sais."* An erased name precedes this title, and was probably that of a Shepherd-King.

Assa was succeeded by Aphôbis, according to Africanus. Josephus calls this King Apôphis. His name is not found on the monuments.

* See Plate VII., No. 14.

Many writers of modern times have rejected all the remarkable traditions of the ancient Greeks respecting their early connexion with Egypt, as undeserving of the serious consideration of the learned. That there is much of fable in the early Greek traditions, cannot be denied; but it is as certain, in my opinion, that there is much truth, respecting the colonization of Greece, contained in those traditions, upon which I must here remark. All the traditions of a nation are not necessarily false because mixed up with mythological fables.

The origin of the several Greek Kingdoms is involved in great obscurity. It has been supposed that that of Sicyon commenced in the twenty-first century B.C.; and that of Argos, about the middle of the nineteenth century B.C. About the latter time, we find traces of the connexion between Greece and Egypt, which are nowhere more evident than in the legend of Io, the daughter of Inachus. The most remarkable of the colonizing tribes were the Pelasgi; whose name, unfortunately, does not enable us to say what was their race. Homer makes mention of them as auxiliaries of the Trojans, coming from Larissa*. With respect to this and the other tribes which colonized Greece, for they must have been several tribes, not one, of which the Greek traditions speak, one thing is certain; that these traditions make them either Egyptians or a people intimately connected with Egypt and Palestine. It is evident, also, that the ancient Greeks made no distinction between the Egyptians and the Shepherds. We also find that they knew nothing of the previous history of these tribes; or rather, nothing more than that they came from Egypt or Phœnicia. This is shown by

---

* Iliad, B. II., v. 840, 841.

the confusion of personifications with persons. The traditions respecting Danaus furnish an example of this. He is called the brother of Ægyptus, and son of Belus, and, by his mother, the grandson of Nilus. Belus is a mythical personage, a deified traditional King of the Babylonians; and here it seems probable that he typifies a race. From the time at which the migrations from Egypt to Greece occurred, and from other circumstances, I can entertain no doubt that the greater number of the migrating people were of the tribes which the Egyptians called Shepherds. This opinion seems to be confirmed by their being connected, not only with Egypt, but also, with Phœnicia; for many of the Shepherds were evidently Phœnicians settled in Egypt. Some of the colonizers of Greece, however, may have come directly from Phœnicia.

After the termination of the Twelfth Dynasty, the Diospolite Kingdom was ruled by the Thirteenth, which was contemporary with part of the Fifteenth and Sixteenth Dynasties, and with the whole of the Seventeenth, supposing the Sixteenth to have commenced before the conclusion of the Twelfth; and it was also contemporary with the Eighth Dynasty of Memphites, and part of the Ninth, and the whole of the Tenth, of Heracleopolites, and probably with the greater part of the Fourteenth Dynasty, of Xoites.

The Thirteenth Dynasty commenced towards the conclusion of the twentieth century B.C., or early in the nineteenth century. Africanus and Eusebius agree in assigning to this Dynasty sixty Kings and a duration of 453 years: but the interval from the conclusion of the Twelfth Dynasty to the commencement of the Eighteenth Dynasty is about four hundred years, or somewhat less; and consequently it is evident that the duration assigned to the Thirteenth Dynasty is too long. In the list of the Chamber of Kings, we find thirty royal names (including effaced rings) in the right half, which are the prenomens of the Kings of this Dynasty. The last King's ring in the left half, No. 31, and doubtless the effaced ring immediately preceding it, should likewise be referred to this Dynasty; so that the list altogether contains thirty-two names of Kings of the Thirteenth Dynasty; but probably there were more, who were usurpers. It may, however, be asked, What reason is there for concluding that the last thirty-two Kings of the list of the Chamber of Kings belong to Manetho's Thirteenth Dynasty? That they are Diospolites is shown by their prenomens being always given, and not their nomens. Moreover, such of their names as are found on the monuments are only found in Upper Egypt and Ethiopia. Lastly, it is satisfactorily ascertained that they were after the Twelfth Dynasty. Therefore, as there is no Diospolite Dynasty but the Thirteenth after the Twelfth, we cannot hesitate to refer these Kings to that Dynasty. I am aware that some have followed Eusebius in making two of the Shepherd-Dynasties to be Dynasties of Diospolites or Thebans; but it is evident that Eusebius's version of the lists is here inaccurate. Africanus makes the Seventeenth Dynasty, as I have before mentioned, a Dynasty of Thebans and Shepherds. If he be correct, then what I have called the Thirteenth Dynasty must be the Thirteenth together with the Diospolites of the Seventeenth. But this I think very improbable, and therefore I adopt the opinion before expressed.

The nomens of the Kings of the Thirteenth Dynasty which have been found are mostly Sebak-hotp and

Nufre-hotp. Doubtless most of these Kings, if not all of them, were tributary to the Shepherds, and probably were often set up and put down by them. In the table of the hieroglyphic names of the Kings of the first seventeen Dynasties at the end of this volume, I have placed the names of the Kings of the Thirteenth Dynasty in the order which I think most probably correct.

The Xoite Kingdom, whose Kings composed the Fourteenth Dynasty, probably commenced with, or during, the Twelfth Dynasty. Africanus and Eusebius agree in assigning to it seventy-six Kings. The former states that they reigned 184 years; and the latter, 184 or 484. If the number of Kings be correct, most probably the longer sum is correct also.

The Fifteenth Dynasty seems to have concluded early in the eighteenth century B.C., and was succeeded by Memphite Kings. I am unable to decide whether the Seventh Dynasty succeeded the Sixth and preceded the Fifteenth, or succeeded the Fifteenth and preceded the Eighth, as I have already said. According to Africanus, the Eighth Dynasty ruled for 146 years, and consisted of twenty-seven Kings. I have not been able to ascertain any of its Kings with certainty among those whose hieroglyphic names have been found. In the lists, we do not find the names of any of them.

I have nothing to add to what I have already said respecting the Sixteenth and Seventeenth Dynasties, but that only one of their Kings, Snufre, of the Sixteenth Dynasty, who was a contemporary of Amenemha III., has been identified by me among the Kings mentioned on the monuments.

I have now to consider the latter part of the Shepherd-period, the most remarkable events of which are

182   ETYMOLOGY OF   [Part II.

the commencement of the great Shepherd-war of expulsion, and the numerous migrations from Egypt to other countries.

I broke off the citation of Manetho's account of the Shepherds at the death of Salatis. After relating that event, the historian gives the durations of the reigns of his successors; and adds, "And these six were their first rulers, [and were] ever warring against the Egyptians, and desiring much to root out the race." (ποθοῦντες μᾶλλον τῆς Αἰγύπτου ἐξᾶραι τὴν ῥίζαν.) It is evident, however, that the policy of the Shepherd-Kings of the Fifteenth Dynasty was not such as is here represented. The statement would, I think, be far more applicable to the Shepherd-Kings of the period after the Fifteenth Dynasty. What follows is quite as much to the purpose here as in the examination of the earlier portion of the Shepherd-history, especially as statements respecting the origin of the Shepherd-tribes are now to be considered.—Manetho, according to Josephus, continues thus:—"All this nation of them was called "Hyksôs," ('Τκσὼs,) that is, "Shepherd-Kings;" for "Hyk" ("Τκ) in the sacred dialect signifies "a King," and "Sôs" (Σὼs) is "a shepherd" and "shepherds" in the vulgar dialect; and thus is [the term] Hyksôs composed. And some say that they were Arabs."—We find in hieroglyphics, that one of the names for King is "hak," but we do not find any word like sôs; though in Coptic, ϣⲱⲥ signifies "a shepherd." It seems strange, however, that a tribe or nation should be called Shepherd-Kings; and I am inclined to adopt another etymology, which I shall presently notice. The statement that the Shepherds, according to some, were Arabs, is important, especially as corroborating a curious statement of the Greek writers which I shall likewise soon have to mention. Perhaps the whole passage which I have last cited is not an extract from Manetho's work, but merely an abstract of what he states: what immediately follows is certainly in the words of Josephus; and perhaps the portion stating that some said that the Shepherds were Arabs is also inserted by Josephus, and not from Manetho. We must always bear in mind that the Shepherds were evidently a mixed race of many different nations or tribes; and all that we can say is, that it appears that some of them were Phœnicians; others, Arabs; (probably of several tribes;) and that the first ruler of the Shepherds, and most of his troops, seem to have been Phœnicians, and were perhaps of Tyre.

Josephus, before continuing his abstract or citation of Manetho's account of the Shepherds in Egypt, mentions another etymology of Hyksôs, founded on a signification of " Hyk " and " Hak " in Egyptian; namely, " captives;" so that the name would read " captive Shepherds;" and this he tells us was found in another copy of Manetho. Josephus adds, that this etymology appeared to be more credible and consistent with ancient history. Further on, he says, " In another book of the Ægyptiaca, Manetho says that this nation, which was called the Shepherds, was said in their sacred books to be captives." In hieroglyphics, " Huk " signifies " a captive;" and I think, therefore, that the name " Hyksôs " signified " captive," meaning " foreign, Shepherds." From the circumstance that " sôs " was a term of the vulgar dialect, it is probable that the name " Hyksôs " was never written in hieroglyphics; and hence, probably, arose the different explanations of its signification; but it should be observed that, in hieroglyphics, *foreign enemies* are frequently represented as *captives*.

Josephus then continues, " These above-mentioned Kings of those who were called Shepherds, and their successors, ruled Egypt, he says, for five hundred and eleven years. And he says that, after this, the Kings of the Thebaïd and of the rest of Egypt made an insurrection against the Shepherds, and a great and long war raged between them." This statement shows the date of the commencement of the great Shepherd-war to have been about half a century before the beginning of the Eighteenth Dynasty, if the Fifteenth Dynasty commenced early in the twenty-first century B.C. "The Kings of the Thebaïd and of the rest of Egypt" were evidently of the Thirteenth Dynasty, and of the Fourteenth, and perhaps of the Tenth also.

At this point I should have concluded the present section if I were to restrict it to the period of the Shepherd-domination, which I have no doubt terminated some time before the commencement of the Eighteenth Dynasty; but as the commencement of that Dynasty, also a remarkable point of ancient Egyptian history, is intimately connected with the revolt against the Shepherds, I have thought it best to extend this section somewhat beyond its strict limits, beginning the next with the Eighteenth Dynasty.

It would be interesting could we trace the causes which led to the throwing off the Shepherd-yoke, but unfortunately we have not sufficient information to enable us to do so. Of the period that intervened between the reign of Assa, the last King but one of the Fifteenth Dynasty, and the beginning of the Eighteenth Dynasty, no temples remain, and we have scarcely any records, indicating that it was a time of great adversity to the Egyptians.

It only remains for me to comment upon the accounts transmitted to us by ancient authors of the migrations from Egypt to Greece, which appear to have occurred subsequently to the conclusion of the Fifteenth Dynasty and before the commencement of the Eighteenth, or not long after the latter date. I have reserved this examination to introduce it in the present place because the dates of these successive migrations to Greece are so doubtful, that it is impossible to assign them to any particular periods with exactitude.

The traditions of the ancient Greeks make mention of a great influx of foreigners into Greece during a period extending from about the end of the seventeenth, to about the middle of the fifteenth, century B.C.; the period of Deucalion, Hellen, Cecrops, Cadmus, and Danaus. The conclusion of the interval I place about the middle of the fifteenth century B.C., since that is near the latest date that has been assigned to the coming of Danaus into Greece, the last remarkable event of this period.

The first remarkable event of this interval was the founding of Athens by "Cecrops the Saïte," which is usually referred to the middle or earlier part of the sixteenth century B.C. He is said to have named his city after "Athena," or Minerva, whom all allow to have been the "Neith" of the Egyptians, the goddess of Saïs. Some say that Athens was named in later times. I have already shown, in illustrating the history of the Fifteenth Dynasty, that Saïs was probably one of the cities of the Shepherds in the reign of one of the later Kings of that Dynasty.

The next leader of the colonizers, who is conspicuously mentioned in the traditions, is Cadmus, the founder of Bœotian Thebes. Respecting him there are different narrations; some saying that he came from Phœnicia; and others, from Egypt. In the narrative of the Exodus given by Diodorus, Cadmus, as well as Danaus, is made a leader of the Shepherds, leaving Egypt at the time that Moses and the Israelites came out. Perhaps Cadmus was of a tribe of Phœnicians settled in Egypt, or a leader of an offshoot from a colony of Shepherds which had left Egypt and settled in Phœnicia.

Danaus, according to the account of the Exodus given by Diodorus Siculus, as I have just remarked, was one of the Shepherd-chiefs. That he left Egypt and came to Greece, is universally stated by the ancient writers who relate his traditional history. Manetho calls him "Armaïs, the brother of Sethôsis," whom he identifies with Ægyptus; and he gives an account of the offences for which he was obliged to leave Egypt. Sethôsis, or Sethôs, the Sethee I. of the monuments, and first King of the Nineteenth Dynasty, cannot be Ægyptus; and therefore Manetho is evidently wrong in identifying his brother Armaïs, whose hieroglyphic name has not yet been found, with Danaus. Herodotus and Diodorus Siculus say that the brother of Sesôstris plotted against him on his return from conquest, evidently speaking of the person called by Manetho Armaïs. It is especially worthy of notice that, according to Herodotus, King Amasis, of the Twenty-sixth Dynasty, made gifts to the temple of Minerva at Lindus, because it was said to have been built by the daughters of Danaus, when they fled from the sons of Ægyptus*.

* Herodotus, II., 182.

ORIGIN OF THE SHEPHERDS.

Respecting the origin of Cadmus and the colonists of his time, Strabo* tells us, that the Euboeans were Arabs who passed over with Cadmus; and Agatharchides† and Diodorus Siculus‡ relate, that a tribe of Arabs called by the former Dedebæ, and by the latter Debæ, were very hospitable to the Bœotians and Peloponnesians, from a mythos concerning Hercules, which, Diodorus says, they had preserved in a tradition. This reminds us of what is said in the first Book of Maccabees; that the Lacedæmonians claimed affinity with the Jews. It seems to me, that, although it is not to be inferred that these Arabs mentioned by Diodorus and Agatharchides were of the same race as the Peloponnesians and Bœotians, yet, probably, their progenitors left Egypt together, or during the same period; and this view is, I think, strengthened by the case of the Jews and Lacedæmonians; for it is highly probable that the Lacedæmonians supposed the Jews to have been of a kindred origin with themselves from a tradition relating that the progenitors of both nations left Egypt about the same time. In saying this I do not allude to the Bible-narrative; but it is worthy of remark that the people called in our version "a mixed multitude," who went out from Egypt with the Israelites are called in the Hebrew original by a name which I have no doubt signifies Arabs. (Compare Jer. XXV. 24.) Upon the whole it appears to me evident that some of the Shepherds were Arabs, and I have already shewn that some of them were Phœnicians.

* Geog. lib. x., p. 447.
† De Rubr. Mar., p. 59, ap. Hudson.
‡ Bibl. Hist. l. iii., c. 44.

SECTION V.

HISTORY OF THE PERIOD OF THE EIGHTEENTH AND NINETEENTH DYNASTIES.

I HAVE now to consider the most brilliant period of Egyptian history, the rule of the Eighteenth and Nineteenth Dynasties, during which the kingdom rapidly rose in power, until the nations of Asia and Africa, from the Tigris to Abyssinia, became tributary states under the control of the Pharaohs. A complete examination of Manetho's lists and the monumental history of these Dynasties would fill volumes; and therefore I shall chiefly confine myself, in the present work, to certain remarkable points upon which I conceive new light may be thrown, and to the chronology of the period.

I shall first give a table of the Eighteenth and Nineteenth Dynasties according to the lists of Manetho.

TABLE OF MANETHO'S LISTS OF THE EIGHTEENTH AND NINETEENTH DYNASTIES.

Dyn.	No.	JOSEPHUS.	Yrs.	M.	No.	AFRICANUS.		No.	EUSEBIUS.	Years. Gr.	Arm.
18	1.	Tethmôsis	25	4	1.	Amôs	13	1.	Amôsis	25	25
	2.	Chebrôn	13		2.	Chebrôs	24	2.	Chebrôn	13	13
	3.	Amenôphis	20	7	3.	Amenôphthis	22	3.	Ammenôphis	21	21
	4.	Amessés	21	9	4.	Amensis	13				
	5.	Méphrés	12	9	5.	Misaphris	26	4.	Miphrés	12	12
	6.	Mephramuthôsis	25	10	6.	Misphragmuthôsis	9	5.	Misphragmuthôsis	26	26
	7.	Thmôsis	9	8	7.	Tuthmôsis	31	6.	Tuthmôsis	9	9
	8.	Amenôphis	30	10	8.	Amenôphis	37	7.	Amenôphis	31	31
	9.	Ôros	36	5	9.	Ôros	32	8.	Ôros	36 / 38	28
	10.	Akenchrés	12	1	10.	Acherrés	6	9.	Achenchersés	16 / 12	16
	11.	Rathôtis	9		11.	Rathôs	12	10.	Acherrés	8	8
	12.	Akenchérés	12	5	12.	Chebrés	12	11.	Cherrés	15	15
	13.	Akenchérés	12	3	13.	Acherrés	5				
	14.	Armais	4	1	14.	Armessés	1	12.	Armais	5	5
	15.	Ramessés	1	4	15.	Ramessés					
	16.	Armessés Miammû	66	2	16.	Amenôphath	19	13.	Ramessés	68	68
	17.	Amenôphis	19	6	1.	Sethôs	51	14.	Amenôphis	40	40
19	1.	Sethôsis-Ramessés	59		2.	Rapsakés	61	1.	Sethôs	55	55
	2.	Rampsés	66		3.	Amenephthés	20	2.	Rampsés	66	66
					4.	Ramessés	60	3.	Ammenephthis	40	8
					5.	Ammenemnés	5	4.	Ammenemés	26	26
					6.	Thuôris	7	5.	Thuôris	7	7

I must now shew what corrections and alterations the monuments authorize our making in this list. For greater convenience, I divide the two Dynasties into three parts; the first containing nine sovereigns; the second, five; and the third, eight; according to Africanus's list. Having already given the principal variations of each name, I shall in future only give that orthography which appears most agreeable with the hieroglyphics.

The first King of the Dynasty, Amôsis, is called on the monuments "Aah-mes": the second, Chebrôn,

is not found; and it appears that the third, Amenôphis, or Amenoph I., immediately succeeded Aah-mes. Pos-

sibly Chebrôn was a colleague of Aah-mes or of Amenoph I. It seems to me that we cannot err in excluding him from the regular succession. The fourth sovereign, Queen Amessês, is the Queen "Aah-mes" of the monuments, the Queen of Thothmes I.

Mêphrês is Thothmes II.; and Mephramuthôsis,

Thothmes III. A date of the latter King's thirty-third

year is found in a tablet; and therefore it is evident that twenty-five years and ten months is far too short a reign for him. I think that we may assign to him a reign of thirty-five years and ten months with probability. The hieroglyphic inscriptions shew that Thothmes III. was succeeded by his son Amenoph II., who

reigned at least four years. This King is altogether omitted in Manetho's lists, as they now stand; and this fact, together with the short sum assigned to the reign of Thothmes III., plainly shews that we cannot place reliance upon the numbers of Kings, and the lengths of their reigns, in Manetho's lists, as they now stand, and that our only safe course is to rely wholly upon the dates of the Egyptian monuments, and the historical records of different Kings preserved on them;

adopting, as nearest to the truth, that version of Manetho which agrees best with these dates and records. I wish to place this observation before the reader in the strongest light, and to request his particular attention to it.

The successor of Mephramuthôsis in Manetho's lists, Tuthmôsis, is Thothmes IV.; and his successor,

Amenôphis, Amenoph III.   Sir Gardner Wilkinson*

has found a date of his thirty-sixth year; so that the sum of thirty years and ten months is wrong; and thus the monuments shew that we cannot reckon his reign to have been less than thirty-five years and ten months or thirty-six years and ten months, supposing the number of months to be correct. Ôros, or Horus, is called, on the monuments, "Hor-em-heb."

The five names comprehended in the second division

* Materia Hieroglyphica, Part II., Pl. I.

THE EIGHTEENTH DYNASTY.

do not belong to the regular succession of the Kings of the Eighteenth Dynasty. The monuments give us no authority on which to put a reign or reigns between Horus and Rameses I., the first King of the next division; and they are in immediate succession in the monumental lists. The question then arises, What is the place of these Kings? Are they co-regents of any of the legitimate Kings of this Dynasty? Chiefs of a powerful foreign race, whose history I shall soon have to mention, obtained possession of Egypt for some time during the reign of Hor-em-heb, and, perhaps, during part of the reign of Amenoph III. I cannot doubt that this portion of the list contains the names of the Kings of this foreign race who reigned in Egypt; though identification of all their names is not easy. The most famous of them, " Bekh-en-atenra," is probably an

" Akenchêrês," or " Acherrês." " Hak-ka-ra" is un-

doubtedly an " Acherrês." I shall have to notice these Kings again; and it is only necessary here to remark that their monuments are so much destroyed that we have not the means of correcting or verifying Manetho's numbers as given by the several copyists. There can be little doubt, however, that Africanus's and

Josephus's versions are more correct in this part than Eusebius's, as such is the case in the other parts of the lists.

We have now to consider the third division of the lists of the Eighteenth and Nineteenth Dynasties. There is a remarkable errour in this part of all the lists, which has been already pointed out by others: certain Kings being twice mentioned. This will be made more clear by the following tabular view, in which this portion of the lists is compared with the monuments, the names which are virtually identical being placed opposite to each other.

JOSEPHUS.		AFRICANUS.		EUSEBIUS.		MONUMENTS.
	Yrs.	XVIII. 15, 16.	XIX. 1, 2, 3.	XVIII. 13, 14.	XIX. 1, 2, 3.	
Yrs. M.		Rameses . . 1				
Rameses 1 4			Sethôs . . 51		Sethôs . . 55	Rameses I.
	Sethôsis . 59					Sethee I.
Armesês 66 2	Rampsês . 66		Rapsakês . 61	Ramesês . 68	Rampsês . 66	Rameses II.
Amenô-phis . 19 6		Amenophath 19	Ameneph-thês . . 20	Amenôphis 40	Ammeneph-this 40 or 8	Menptah.

From this it is perfectly clear that certain Kings properly belonging to the Nineteenth Dynasty, and there placed, have been also placed in the Eighteenth, in these lists, after Ramessês, or Rameses I., who should be the last King of the Eighteenth Dynasty, according to Manetho's arrangement. The list should be as follows: Ramessês, (1 4,) or Rameses I.;

Sethôs, or Sethee I.; Rampsês, (66 2,) or Rameses

II.[1]; and Amenephthês, (19 6,) or Menptah[2]. The reign

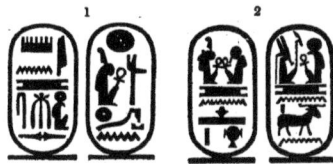

of Sethôs is differently stated by Africanus, Eusebius, and Josephus; but the monuments show it to be probable that they have all assigned to him too long a reign; though the magnitude of the works executed by him show that his reign could not have been short. My reason for supposing that this King did not reign for such a long period as is assigned to him in the lists is, that he is represented as accompanied by his eldest son, (whose name is partly erased, but certainly was not Rameses,) in an expedition which took place in the first year of his reign; and that, in another expedition, without a date, he is represented as accompanied by his son Rameses. The representations to which I allude form a portion of the famous sculptures of the north wall of the great temple of El-Karnak. (See Rosellini's Monumenti Storici, l. and liv. 2.) Manetho says, that Rampsês was the "eldest of the sons" of Sethôs. If, as is most probable, the two names mentioned in the sculptures of the temple of El-Karnak do not apply to one prince, Manetho must mean the eldest surviving son at the time of the death of Sethôs. In either case, the improbability of Sethôs's having reigned between fifty and sixty years is obvious. The Ramessês whom Africanus makes the fourth King of the Nineteenth Dynasty, assigning to him a reign of sixty years, is not mentioned on the monuments, and is undoubtedly spurious, having been probably introduced by an errour of the copyist. Probably Ammenemnês, the next King, is the Amen-meses

of the monuments; and Thuôris, the Menptah Siptah.

Perhaps these two Kings reigned during a period of disturbance in the reign of Menptah; but the monuments do not enable us to decide this question, nor do they tell us which of them reigned first.

We obtain an approximative date of the commencement of the Eighteenth Dynasty from the date in the sixteenth year of Queen Amen-numt. From that date

we find the commencement of the Dynasty to have been about the year B.C. 1525: for it is evident that the reign of Queen Amen-numt commenced with, or was reckoned from, the accession of Thothmes II.; and it is also evident that there is no errour of magnitude in the lengths assigned to the preceding reigns. The commencement of the Nineteenth Dynasty was, I have no doubt, somewhat before the commencement of the first Sothic Cycle, B.C. 1322, and its duration somewhat more than a hundred years. I have said enough to show how impossible it is to fix accurately the length of the reign of each King: and for this and other reasons, we cannot yet attempt to draw out a completely correct list of these Dynasties, the most perplexing of all those of which Manetho's lists have come down to us.

The first remarkable point in the history of the Eighteenth Dynasty, which I have to notice, is the reign of Queen Amen-numt. This personage, whose name is not found in Manetho's lists, reigned conjointly with Thothmes II. and Thothmes III. for some years, treating those Kings as inferiors, and always taking the most honourable position on public occasions, as we know from the many sculptures which she has left. The most extraordinary circumstance connected with her is, that she is always represented as wearing male attire*.

I have now to return for a time to the subject of

* This has suggested to me the possibility that Amen-numt may be a Semiramis, a supposition which is supported by our finding that her date is not far anterior to the approximative date of a Semiramis obtained from the fragments of Berossus. I say "a Semiramis," because the Semiramis of Berossus may be a second Queen of that name; as Rameses II. was called by some Sesôstris after an earlier King. In a Latin list of the Kings of Assyria given by Scaliger, and possibly, as Cory remarks, taken from Castor's Canon, is a second Semiramis, whose accession is dated very near the time of that of Amen-numt. The lists of Assyrian Kings given by Africanus and Eusebius have many points of similarity to this. I have already noticed what Diodorus Siculus says respecting the rule of Semiramis; to which I may add his remark that, according to Ctesias, they who came into Egypt with Semiramis built certain cities. (I. 56.) It is not a little curious, that, in the list of Assyrian Kings given by Africanus, a King of the name of Sethôs occurs eight reigns after Semiramis; and that the reign of Sethee I., whom Manetho calls Sethôs or Sethôsis, is the eighth after that of Amen-numt, reckoning the foreign rule in the time of Horus as one reign: but on this I lay no stress, as this list of Assyrian Kings is suspicious. I offer the suggestion that Amen-numt may be the Egyptian name of a Semiramis with diffidence, as merely hypothetical; and future discoveries may prove or disprove its correctness. If it prove to be correct, we shall understand more of the causes of the changes in Egypt, and the conquests out of Egypt, which commenced about this time. We might find a double line of Kings, Assyrians or Asiatics, and Egyptians, laying claim to the great oriental empire as a right; sometimes ruling it together, and at others independently of each other. We cannot yet decide this question, but it is worthy of a careful examination, as bearing upon the causes of the Egyptian conquests, and illustrating the early history of Egypt and Assyria.

the Shepherds in Egypt, whose Exodus is stated by Manetho to have taken place in the course of this Dynasty. No inscription has hitherto been found on the Egyptian monuments recording this event, or even alluding to it. This silence is, however, easily to be explained. We never find that the Egyptians recorded anything on their monuments which they considered discreditable to their valour; and consequently, we cannot expect to find on them an account of a transaction in which, according to Manetho, an Egyptian army of 480,000 men was unable to reduce a fortified place defended by a garrison of Shepherds of about half their number. Manetho, cited by Josephus, gives an account of the Shepherd-Exodus, and the events which preceded it, in a portion of his history which I have already partly quoted. To quote the remainder in full would be unnecessary; and therefore I shall only give an abstract of it, commencing at the place where I broke off my quotation.

After mentioning the insurrection of the Kings of the Thebaïd and of the rest of Egypt, and the Shepherd-war, Manetho says that, at last, a King called Misphragmuthôsis drove the Shepherds out of all Egypt excepting their stronghold of Avaris. He then proceeds to relate that Thummôsis, the son of Misphragmuthôsis, endeavoured to take Avaris by siege, blockading it with a force of 480,000 men; but finding that he could not take it, he made conditions with the Shepherds, that they should leave Egypt unmolested, for whatever country they desired. And in consequence of this agreement, the Shepherds left Egypt with their families and possessions, in number not less than 240,000, and went into Syria; but fearing the power of the Assyrians, who then ruled Asia, they built, in

Judea, a city sufficient to contain them, and called it Jerusalem.

Here it should be observed, that Manetho, as cited by Josephus, makes Thothmes IV. the King of the Shepherd-Exodus: Josephus, however, also cites from Manetho that the King of the Shepherd-Exodus was the first King of the Eighteenth Dynasty, the Aahmes of the monuments. As the monuments do not enable us to decide this question, I shall not discuss it. We must be careful not to place reliance upon Manetho when the monuments and other ancient records throw no light upon what he relates, as in the present case.

Not long after the time of Thothmes IV., there was a great change in Egypt. A foreign tribe of sun-worshippers settled in that country, and subjugated it; so that for some years it was wholly ruled by them. This seems to have been noticed by Manetho, for Eusebius, in the second part of his Chronicle, mentions that, during the reign of Amenophis, (Amenoph III.,) the seventh sovereign of the Eighteenth Dynasty, according to his list, but in Africanus's the eighth, " the Ethiopians, migrating from the river Indus, came and dwelt near to Egypt;" and in the Catalogue of Kings of Egypt by an anonymous author, given by Syncellus, we find the following sentence immediately before the mention of Òros: " The Ethiopians, coming from the river Indus, settled near to Egypt."* Of course this statement would be of no value if resting solely on the authority of Syncellus; but when we find it also in the Chronicle of Eusebius, it becomes highly probable that it was originally derived from Manetho, though evi-

* Eusebii Chronicon, P. ii., p. 97. ed. Aucher; and Syncelli Chronographia, p. 151.

dently altered by misapprehension. Our finding that Egypt and Ethiopia were under the power of foreign chiefs very near the time mentioned by Eusebius proves the statement which I am considering to be founded on fact.

These Ethiopians are said to have come from the river Indus; and this implies that they belonged to the race which may be called that of the " Eastern Ethiopians." The accounts of ancient authors shew that the Eastern Ethiopians chiefly inhabited Gedrosia and Carmania; and it is probable that their territories did not extend further eastward than the river Indus. Herodotus, in his account of the army of Xerxes, describes them as a lank-haired people, to distinguish them from the Ethiopians of the countries watered by the Upper Nile. The Cuthites, or inhabitants of Cuthah, or Cuth, placed by the King of Assyria in the cities of the ten tribes with inhabitants of Babylon, &c., may be the same people*.

The earliest indication that I have found of the presence of the sun-worshippers in Egypt is of the time of Amenoph III., in an inscription on a scarabæus, with the date of the eleventh year of his reign, in which their god, Aten-ra, or the Solar Disk, is distinctly mentioned, and in a manner which leaves no doubt that it is not simply an Egyptian inscription†. This furnishes us with a strong reason for adopting Sir Gardner Wilkinson's opinion, that Amenoph III. belonged to this race of sun-worshippers. Sir Gardner's reasons for this opinion are, that Amenoph III. is like the foreigners in his features, and unlike Egyptian Kings;

---

* 2 Kings, xvii. 24, 30.
† Rosellini's Monumenti Storici, xliv. 2.

and that Bekh-en-atenra, one of their Kings, is represented worshipping him at Soleb, in Ethiopia. After the reign of Amenoph III., the foreign chiefs became very powerful, and ruled Egypt and Ethiopia for some years. I have already shewn that names which I think apply to these Kings are found in Manetho's list, between Ôros (Hor-em-heb) and Ramessês (Rameses I.) of the Eighteenth Dynasty; and since the former King destroyed their monuments, they must be reckoned as before the latter part of his reign at least; but they were after Thothmes IV., and at least partly after Amenoph III.; and consequently, they must be placed between Amenoph III. and Hor-em-heb, or reckoned as partly contemporary with one or both of them. I believe the latter to have been the case, and that they were chiefly contemporary with Hor-em-heb, since his monuments are few, and thus indicate a much shorter actual reign than that assigned to him by Manetho. Probably Manetho reckons his reign from the termination of that of Amenoph III.

To class the Kings of the sun-worshippers in their proper order is a work of great difficulty; though much has been done by Sir Gardner Wilkinson and M. Prisse towards effecting this desirable object. The most remarkable of them are Bekh-en-atenra and Amen-tu-ankh*. I do not think it certain that Skhee

belonged to this race. If it be proved that he did,

their coming to Egypt must be referred to many years before the reign of Amenoph III.

The monuments erected by the sun-worshippers in Egypt must have been considerable; but few of them now remain, and these have suffered severely from the hatred which the Egyptians bore to those who founded them. Their most remarkable records are to be found in the sculptures and paintings of the grottoes of the ancient town of Psinaula, in the sculptures on the hills near Ashmooneyn, (the old Hermopolis Magna,) and in some sculptures in Ethiopia. From these records we obtain a general idea of their religion, which was a variety of a worship formerly so widely prevalent in Asiatic countries. In their religious sculptures we find the sun represented as a disk, with numerous rays issuing from it, each terminating with a human hand, one of which presents to the worshipper the symbol of life. The names under which this people worshipped the sun are "Aten-ra," or the solar disk, that is, the visible sun; "Muee-ra," the brightness, or rays, of the sun; and "Ra," the power supposed to reside in the sun. We find the names of their god enclosed in two royal rings*, shewing that they ascribed to him a regal character. The names thus enclosed read "Ra of the two solar abodes, who rejoices in the solar abode, in his name Muee-ra, who is in Aten-ra."

It is well known that sun-worship was practised in ancient times by many powerful nations of Asia, by some of the Chaldeans, by the Medes, Persians, and Bactrians, by the Massagetæ, a tribe of the Scythians, and by some of the Syrians. Among all these nations, the sun appears to have been the principal object of

* See Plate VII., No. 15.

worship; and among some of them, the sole god. It is interesting to compare as much as we know concerning the religion of the sun-worshippers in Egypt with the "Chaldean Oracles of Zoroaster," as given by Cory in his "Ancient Fragments." Although many of them must be of late origin, and others must have suffered by translation into Greek, they certainly contain many of the principles of the old religion of Zoroaster. Thus, for example, we read,

"It becomes thee to hasten to the light and *rays* of the Father, From whence was sent to thee a *soul*, endued with much mind."

Χρὴ σε σπεύδειν πρὸς τὸ φάος καὶ πατρὸς αὐγὰς,
Ἔνθεν ἐπέμφθη σοι ψυχὴ, πολὺν ἐσσαμένη νοῦν.

(Anc. Frag., p. 272.)

This sentence presents a curious comment on the worship of the foreigners in Egypt, as represented upon their own monuments; and similar instances might be added; but I shall only notice two other peculiarities. We have already seen the regal character of Aten-ra in the inscriptions of the sun-worshippers in Egypt; and we find the same mentioned in the Oracles, as well as in many fragments and lists of Kings in which we find Belus, the chief god of the Babylonians, as the first King, or an early King. In a curious fragment of Megasthenes, preserved by Eusebius, who found it in the history of the Assyrians by Abydenus, we have an account of a prophecy said to have been delivered by Nebuchadnezzar, (here called Nabuchodrosorus,) who speaks of the approaching conquest of his country by the Medes and Persians as "a calamity which neither Belus my ancestor, nor Queen Beltis, have power to persuade the Fates to avert." (συμφορὴν, τὴν οὔτε Βῆλος ἐμὸς πρόγονος, οὔτε βασίλεια Βῆλτις ἀποτρέψαι μοίρας πεῖσαι σθενοῦσι*.) This passage is curious as identifying the primeval King and the chief god of the Babylonians, and mentioning a female Bel, Queen Beltis.

Zoroaster and his followers (I do not mean those holding the opinions of the Zend-Avesta) generally speak of but one deity, though it is evident that they worshipped a triad or triads, just as the sculptures of the sun-worshippers in Egypt uniformly represent but one object of adoration, although that people, also, evidently worshipped a kind of triad. It appears to me, from the different names given to the god of the sun-worshippers, that they adored one god, whom they supposed to be resident in the sun, and operating through its rays, and yet that they worshipped this god through the medium of the sun and its rays. These evidently correspond to the Fire, the Sun, or Light, and the Ether, of the Zoroastrian triad, originating from a monad†. The only one of these correspondences that appears at first sight strained is that of "Ether," in the Zoroastrian triad, with the god supposed to reside in the sun by the sun-worshippers in Egypt; but the objection is removed when we remember that the Ether of Zoroaster corresponds to the Soul or Spirit of the Universe of some of the ancient theologists and some of the philosophers. How interesting is it to see, in the earliest monuments of Asiatic nations of which the date is proved, the first records of that religion which so widely prevailed in Asia for so many ages, and which is not yet extinct.

Precisely how and when the sun-worshippers were expelled from Egypt does not appear; though it can-

* Anc. Frag., p. 44.
† See the Oracles of Zoroaster, and Cory's Philosophical Inquiry appended to the Ancient Fragments. (Anc. Frag., Second edit., pp. 239-280, and 333 ad. fin.)

not be doubted that Óros, the Hor-em-heb of the monuments, was the King who overcame them; for he succeeded their Kings. It has also been ascertained that he added a portal with wings to the great temple of El-Karnak, constructed of the materials of former edifices erected by the foreign Kings; and this, added to the fact of the very frequent erasure of their names by the Egyptians, makes it probable that they were expelled by force. The Egyptians evidently hated the sun-worshippers, and more especially their Kings, most probably because of the diversity of their religion.

I have already mentioned the statement of Manetho, that Sethôsis, or Sethôs, the Sethee I. of the monuments, was Ægyptus, the brother of Danaus; and I have shewn the historian's mistake in this instance. I have also spoken of the expulsion of a foreign race, apparently of Shepherds, by the same King, in the first year of his reign, from the eastern part of Lower Egypt, recorded on the monuments.

In this portion of the present work, (Part II.,) I have shewn the perfect consistency of the ancient Egyptian Chronology as derived from the lists of the Dynasties, and from their history as found on the monuments, with the Chronology derived from dates of the divisions of time, explained in Part I.

It was my intention to have added a critical examination of the statements of several ancient authors respecting Egyptian Chronology; but as such statements can neither invalidate nor strengthen the evidence of the monuments, and as such an examination could have no better result than to disprove the systems of others, which I have already virtually disproved by the testimony of the monuments, I have determined to omit it.

I end this inquiry with the Nineteenth Dynasty, because the Chronology and History of the subsequent Dynasties are comparatively clear and well known. The great problem that was to be solved was the Chronology and History of the first Seventeen Dynasties, which some have limited to a period of less than six hundred years, and others have extended to about four thousand.

CONCLUDING REMARKS.

I now conclude this work by briefly recapitulating the chief results of the investigations which it contains.

The Sothic Cycle has been long known, but imperfectly understood; and I have explained some very important particulars relating to it, overlooked by others. The Tropical Year, as divided into Three Seasons, was very imperfectly known, and I have clearly defined it. The Vague and Sothic Years were well known; and I have had nothing new to add concerning them, as unconnected with other divisions of time.

The following divisions of time were either altogether unknown or entirely misapprehended before I published my opinions on Egyptian Chronology; and consequently what I have said respecting them is entirely new. These are the Tropical Cycle; the Phœnix Cycle; and all the periods of the Calendar of the Panegyries; namely, the Great Panegyrical Years and Months and Divisions of Months.

The Tropical Year and the Tropical Cycle confirm each other: the Tropical Cycle is confirmed by the Calendar of the Panegyries: the Sothic Cycle is most satisfactorily fixed, as to its commencement and duration: and the Phœnix Cycle rests upon its consistency with the Sothic Cycle, with the Calendar of the Panegyries, and with historical records.

One of the greatest evidences of the truth of a system is the consistency of its component parts. This is the case with the ancient Egyptian divisions of time as here explained; and it should be added that they were discovered by a laborious process, not all at once, nor in regular sequence, but at different times, and often without any aid from previous discovery. These subjects are considered in the First Part of this work.

In the Second Part, I have illustrated the History of the first Nineteen Dynasties from the monuments, and I have applied the Egyptian Chronology to that History, showing their entire consistency. The contemporaneousness of certain of the first Seventeen Dynasties with others of the same portion of Manetho's list is clearly proved by the evidence of coëval monuments. This is the most important fact of this part of the present work; and it shews that no system of Egyptian Chronology but one exactly or nearly the same as that explained in Part I. can be correct. The discovery that the commencement of the first Great Panegyrical Year B.C. 2717 is the Era of Mênês, the first King of Egypt, ranks next to this in importance. I may also particularize the explanation for the first time of the upper line of the Tablet of Abydos, and of the whole of the List of the Chamber of Kings. I might mention many other subjects upon which I have thrown new light, but these will suffice. If the reader will compare the results of my studies with the statements of ancient authors, he will find many points of agreement, some of which I have had occasion to point out, especially in the cases of Herodotus and Manetho. But what is far more important and interesting, is the fact that these results vindicate the Bible, shewing that the monuments of Egypt in no manner, on no point, contradict that sacred book, but confirm it.

Some have asserted that they disprove the Bible; and others have insinuated that they weaken its authority. The monuments completely disprove both these ideas; and their venerable records most forcibly warn us, not only against the disbelief of Sacred History, but also against distrusting too much the narratives of ancient Profane History, and even Tradition.

It was my intention to have inserted in the present work an examination of the history of the Israelites in Egypt, and of the date of the Exodus; but I have been induced to omit these subjects, and to confine myself, as much as possible, to the Chronology and History obtained from the ancient Egyptian monuments.

APPENDIX.

APPENDIX.

LETTER FROM THE ASTRONOMER ROYAL, IN REPLY TO ONE FROM THE AUTHOR OF THE PRESENT WORK.

Royal Observatory, Greenwich,
April 26, 1850.

SIR,

I AM enabled now to give you the result of calculations applying to the questions proposed in your letter of the 15th instant, with accuracy greater than is required in such investigations. The form of these computations is somewhat unusual to my assistants, and some delay has therefore been occasioned by the necessity of my looking to the calculations myself.

The modern places of the stars have been converted into longitude and latitude, they have then been carried backwards by a process which necessarily includes their proper motions, and then with the proper values of obliquity they have been reconverted into right ascensions and north polar distances. This process is rigorously accurate.

The places of the Sun have been computed by Delambre's Tables, applying the equation of the center. All the equations omitted would not produce 1 minute of arc in the Sun's place. The calculations have been checked by computations from Carlini's Tables. The results of Carlini's (which are probably the more accurate) differ 3 or 4 minutes from Delambre's: but I have preferred to retain Delambre's because they are given for the Paris midnight commencing the civil day, for which time also my lunar places are computed.

The places of the Moon have been computed from Damoiseau's Tables, applying the five principal equations (equation of center, evection, variation, annual equation, reduction for inclination). The equations omitted may perhaps amount to 5 or 6 minutes. The time is the Paris midnight commencing the civil day.

The following is the first set of results:—
I. Obliquity of Ecliptic.

No. (1.) 1322 B.C. . . . . . . 23° 54′ 32″
    (2.) 1985 B.C. . . . . . . 24° 0′ 6″

II. Places of Stars.

(1.) 1322 B.C., Sirius, R.A. . . 4ʰ 19ᵐ 25ˢ, N.P.D. 107° 42′ 13″
(2.) 1985 B.C., α Aquilæ, R.A. . 16ʰ 36ᵐ 34ˢ N.P.D. 82° 49′ 46″

III. Longitudes of the Sun, at Paris midnight commencing the civil day.

(1.) 1322 B.C., July 20 . . . . . . 103° 23′ 41″
(2.) 1985 B.C., January 2 . . . . . 265° 26′ 42″
(3.) 2005 B.C., April 8 . . . . . . 0° 29′ 47″
(4.) 506 B.C., March 27. . . . . . 359° 37′ 32″
(5.) 1652 B.C., April 21 . . . . . . 15° 23′ 25″

IV. Longitudes and approximate Latitudes of the Moon, at Paris midnight commencing the civil day.

(3.) 2005 B.C., April 8, Long. 357° 4′ 56″, Lat. 59′ South, increasing.
(4.) 506 B.C., Mar. 27, Long. 342° 37′ 49″, Lat. 58′ North, increasing.
(5.) 1652 B.C., April 21, Long. 194° 49′ 39″, Lat. 1° 33′ North, increasing.

To the Sun's longitude in No. (1) I have added 7′, and to that in No. (2) I have added 13′, as a rough allowance from midnight at Paris to sunrise at Thebes: and from the altered places I get the following:—

V. Sun's R.A. and N.P.D. at sunrise.

(1.) 1322 B.C., July 20, R.A. 6ʰ 58ᵐ 55ˢ, N.P.D. 66° 47′ 32″.
(2.) 1985 B.C., Jan. 2, R.A. 17ʰ 41ᵐ 1ˢ, N.P.D. 113° 55′ 43″.

VI. With these, and the star-places above, and the latitude of Thebes 25° 44′ North, the following times of rising are computed—

(1.) 1322 B.C., July 20:—
  Sidereal time of sunrise 0ʰ 11ᵐ 12ˢ
  Sidereal time of rising of Sirius. . . . 22ʰ 54ᵐ 49ˢ

    Sirius earlier by 1ʰ 16ᵐ 23ˢ

(2.) 1985 B.C., Jan. 2:—
  Sidereal time of sunrise 12ʰ 40ᵐ 25ˢ
  Sidereal time of rising of α Aquilæ . . 10ʰ 22ᵐ 40ˢ

    α Aquilæ earlier by 2ʰ 17ᵐ 45ˢ

The comparison of the numbers under III. and IV. gives the following:—

VII. Relative positions of the Sun and Moon.

(3.) 2005 B.C., April 8, beginning of civil day,
Moon's longitude . . . . . . 357° 4' 56"
Sun's   ,, ...   0° 29' 47"
                                    ─────────────
Moon *behind* Sun . . . . . .   3° 24' 51"

The true conjunction would therefore be about 6ʰ A.M. at Paris, or about 8ʰ A.M at Thebes.

The true equinox was on the preceding day.

(4.) 506 B.C., March 27, beginning of civil day,
Moon's longitude . . . . . . 342° 37' 49"
Sun's   ,, ... 359° 37' 32"
                                  ─────────────
Moon *behind* Sun . . . . . .   16° 59' 43"

March 27 is the day of the equinox: but the conjunction will not take place till March 28, in the morning.

(5.) 1652 B.C., April 21, beginning of civil day *,
Moon's longitude . . . . . . 194° 49' 39"
Sun's longitude + 180° . . . . . 195° 23' 25"
                                  ─────────────
Moon behind opposition . . . . .   0° 33' 46"

The full moon occurs shortly after Paris midnight (*i. e.* very early in the morning of April 21).

No eclipse at either of these times.

* * * * *

(Signed)   G. B. AIRY.

---

* This calculation refers to my date of the Exodus, which I intended to discuss in the present work at the time that I applied to the Astronomer Royal. R. S. P.

HIEROGLYPHIC TABLES OF KINGS.

THE following tables comprise the names of all the Kings whose chronological places I consider certain, from the First Dynasty to the Nineteenth, Dynasty inclusive. I have, in these tables, arranged the Dynasties and Kings in their proper relative places, according to the authority of the monuments. The spaces allotted to particular Kings are proportioned to the lengths of their reigns only in some particular and remarkable cases: in other cases I have only indicated the average length deduced from the length of the Dynasty and the number of its Kings. The names in these tables, with few exceptions, are printed from wood-blocks of which the use has been most kindly offered to me, for this purpose, by Sir Gardner Wilkinson.

SOME NAMES OF UNPLACED KINGS,

AND SOME

VARIATIONS OF THE NAMES OF PLACED KINGS.

THE following List contains the names of some of those ancient Pharaohs whose places in the first Nineteen Dynasties have not been ascertained, and some variations of names given in the preceding Tables. I subjoin a few particulars respecting these Kings.

1. Name and square title of an ancient Memphite King found in the Great Pyramid of Sakkárah, in the Memphite burial-ground. The name reads Nub-rekhee-ra, "the Sun of pure gold," and resembles the "Χνοῦβος Γνευρὸς ὅ ἐστιν Χρύσης Χρύσου υἱὸς" of the list of Eratosthenes, both in sound and signification. In that list, Chnûbos Gneuros is made the third predecessor of the first Saôphis, the Sûphis I. of Manetho. Χρύσης, the proper name, doubtless signifies "golden," though the Lexicons only say that it is a derivative of χρυσος. It must not be supposed, that, in the translation of Nub-rekhee-ra, I have written "sun" inadvertently for "son." It appears to me to be not improbable that the hieroglyphic name in question may be that of Necherôphês (Afr.), or Necherôchis (Eus.), the first King of the Third Dynasty. I may mention the very ancient character of the inscription containing the name; and in particular the fact, that the royal ring (here circular, not elongated,) follows, instead of enclosing, the name; as favouring this opinion. It may be urged against it, that there would be a considerable gap between this inscription and the next that has been found with a royal name.

2. A name found at Wádee Maghárah. It reads ". . . kau-hor," the sound of one character not being known. Similar names are found in the Fourth and Fifth Dynasties.

3. Name of a King of the Ninth Dynasty, or of the Fourteenth, contemporary with Amenemha III. See pp. 162, 3.

4. A name found with that of Amenemha III. From its form we must conclude it to be a prenomen, unless the King who bore it had but one name.

5. A variation of the prenomen of the ninth King of the Thirteenth Dynasty, according to the order of the list of the Chamber of Kings, as explained by me, found with his nomen.

6 & 7. Prenomens resembling those of the Thirteenth Dynasty, and probably of Kings of that Dynasty: the latter is given by Sir Gardner Wilkinson (Materia Hieroglyphica, p. 117; and Part II. Plate V. F. & G.), as found with another unplaced King (No. 19), whose prenomen resembles those of Kings of the Eighteenth Dynasty, and of the Sun-worshippers contemporary with them.

8 & 9. Prenomen and nomen of a Nufre-hotp, of the Thirteenth Dynasty: in No. 9 both names are enclosed in one ring.

10 & 11. Prenomens, probably of the time of the Thirteenth Dynasty, but, perhaps, more ancient.

12. Prenomen and nomen of the time of the Thirteenth Dynasty, and most probably of a King of that Dynasty, from a tablet in the possession of Mr. A. C. Harris of Alexandria.

13. A very old name found in a grotto at Asyoot, the ancient Lycopolis: whether it be a nomen or prenomen is uncertain: it reads Ka-mee-ra. There is a prenomen resembling it in the List of the Chamber of Kings, that of the sixteenth King of the Thirteenth Dynasty, according to that list, as arranged by me. The difference between the two names is the same as that between Men-ka-ra of the Second Dynasty and Men-kau-ra of the Fourth, and that between the prenomen of Thothmes III. and that of Thothmes IV. Perhaps the Asyoot name is a prenomen of the time of the Thirteenth Dynasty. It is worthy of notice, that an inscription of this King's speaks of the Royal Panegyries, which we do not find mentioned on monuments of the date of which we are certain before the reign of Papa, of the Sixth Dynasty; so that it is possible that this King was not anterior in time to Papa: but in cases of this kind the paucity of monuments prevents our coming to satisfactory conclusions.

14. Perhaps a variation of the prenomen of the fifth King of the Eleventh Dynasty according to the List of the Chamber of Kings.

15, 16, 17. Names of Kings in a series of royal personages, male and female, sculptured in a tomb at Thebes. The only other

King's names, besides the names of Aahmes and Amenoph I., are those of the seventh King of the Eleventh Dynasty, according to the List of the Chamber of Kings. No. 15 is supposed to be the same King as the third King of the Eleventh Dynasty, according to the same list. His nomen, as here written, reads Men-em-hotp.

No. 18 was found by Sir Gardner Wilkinson with the name of Amenoph I., in a tomb at Thebes. The nomen resembles the nomens of Kings of the Eighteenth Dynasty, particularly Horus, and that of the King, commonly held to be Amyrtæus, whose sarcophagus is in the British Museum.

No. 19 has been found with No. 7, as already mentioned.

No. 20. Variation of the nomen of Skhee.

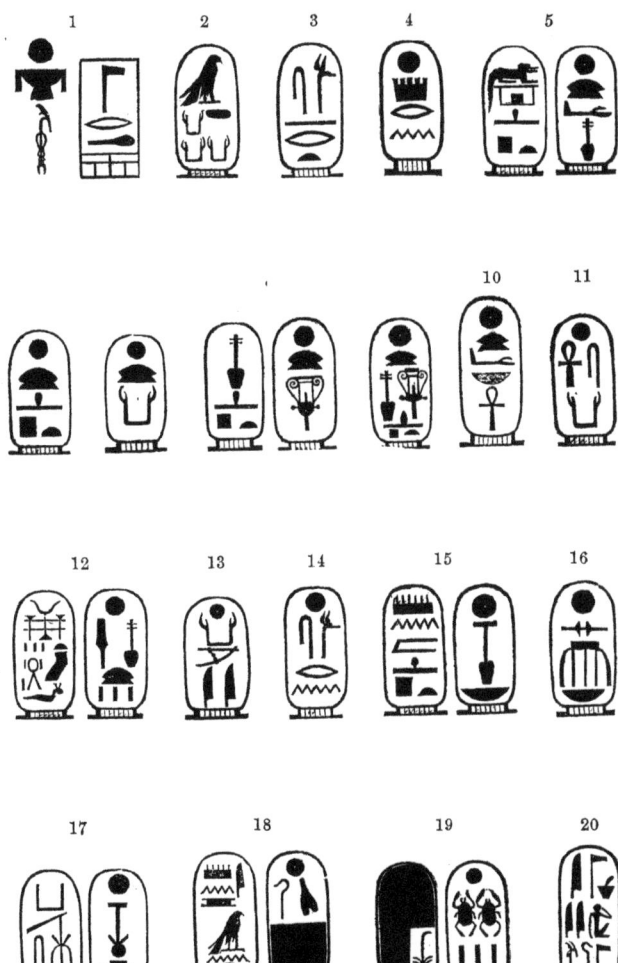

G. Woodfall and Son, Printers, Angel Court, Skinner Street, London.

www.ingramcontent.com/pod-product-compliance
Lightning Source LLC
Chambersburg PA
CBHW040406110426
42812CB00011B/2466